John K.B. Ford & Graeme M. Ellis

Transients

Mammal-Hunting Killer Whales of British Columbia, Washington, and Southeastern Alaska

UBC Press / Vancouver
University of Washington Press / Seattle

Printed in Canada on acid-free paper

ISBN 0-7748-0717-2

Canadian Cataloguing in Publication Data

Ford, John Kenneth Baker, 1955
   Transients

   ISBN 0-7748-0717-2

   Includes bibliographical references.
   ISBN 0-7748-0717-2

   1. Killer whale – Northwest Coast of North America. I. Ellis, Graeme. II. Title.

QL737.C432F67 1999   599.5'36   C99-910140-4

UBC Press gratefully acknowledges the ongoing support to its publishing program from the Canada Council for the Arts, the British Columbia Arts Council, and the Department of Canadian Heritage of the Government of Canada.

Set in Frutiger and Minion
Cartography: Eric Leinberger
Design: George Vaitkunas

UBC Press
University of British Columbia
6344 Memorial Road
Vancouver, BC V6T 1Z2
(604) 822-5959
Fax: 1-800-668-0821
E-mail: orders@ubcpress.ubc.ca
www.ubcpress.ubc.ca

Published simultaneously in the United States of America by the University of Washington Press, P.O. Box 50096, Seattle, WA 98145-5096.

ISBN 0-295-97817-1

Library of Congress Cataloging-in-Publication Data

Ford, John K.B.
   Transients: mammal-hunting killer whales of British Columbia, Washington, and Southeastern Alaska / John K.B. Ford & Graeme M. Ellis.
      p. cm.
   Includes bibliographical references.
   ISBN 0-295-97817-1 (alk. paper)
   1. Killer whale – British Columbia. 2. Killer whale – Washington (State). 3. Killer whale – Alaska. I. Ellis, Graeme M. II. Title.

QL737.C432F675   1999
599.53'617743 – dc21   99-18793
                                         CIP

Published in cooperation with the Vancouver Aquarium Marine Science Centre and the Pacific Biological Station, Department of Fisheries and Oceans, Nanaimo, BC.

 Fisheries and Oceans Pêches et Océans
Canada   Canada
Science   Sciences

Page 2: Transient whale T153 swimming with companion, Queen Charlotte Strait, BC.
C. Tulloch

Contents

Preface and Acknowledgments

Killer whales are one of the most keenly sought and avidly watched species of marine wildlife in the world. Although found in all oceans, nowhere are they better known than in the coastal waters of British Columbia, Washington, and southeastern Alaska. Here in protected seas the whales are easily and reliably found, and whale enthusiasts from around the world come each year in hopes of catching a glimpse of these dramatic predators. The accessibility and predictability of killer whales in these waters is also the reason why much of our scientific knowledge about the species *Orcinus orca* has been learned in this region. Intensive field studies, covering virtually every aspect of killer whale natural history and behaviour that can be studied from a small boat or from shore, have been under way since the early 1970s.

The foremost pioneer of killer whale research was the late Dr. Michael Bigg, a scientist with the Canadian Department of Fisheries and Oceans. In 1970, Mike Bigg took on the task of determining the population status and dynamics of killer whales in British Columbia. At the time, killer whales were being live-captured from local waters in considerable numbers for display in aquaria, yet nothing was known about their abundance in the region. Early in his study, Mike Bigg devised a new technique that would become by far the most important tool in field research on killer whales – photographic identification of individuals. Mike determined that every whale could be positively identified from naturally occurring nicks and scars on its dorsal fin and the grey "saddle patch" at the base of the fin. By photographing and cataloguing every whale, the population could be accurately counted, rather than just estimated, and other important life history parameters could be documented. Despite initial skepticism from some whale biologists, Mike recognized the potential of the photo-identification technique and pursued it vigorously. It is due to Mike Bigg's foresight that so much is understood about killer whale biology today.

By the mid-1970s, Mike Bigg, working together with one of us (Graeme Ellis) and several other biologists, had logged hundreds of encounters with killer whale groups around Vancouver Island and had collected thousands of photographs of dorsal fins. The photo-identifications started to yield some interesting results. Most encounters involved repeated sightings of the same groups of 10 to 30 individual whales. These stable groups, known as *pods*, were found reliably during summer in certain locations off southern and eastern Vancouver Island, particularly in Johnstone Strait and Haro Strait. These pods had quite predictable routines, moving from headland to headland and foraging in tide rips and other good feeding spots. Because of the common presence of these pods and their obvious familiarity with local waters, they were named *residents*.

Occasionally during this early period, the Bigg team encountered small groups of whales or lone individuals that seemed not to be part of the resident communities. These whales were curiosities in many respects. They were seldom seen in groups of more than three or four, and they never mixed with the resident whales. Rather than swimming predictable courses, these "ratty little groups," as Mike Bigg sometimes called them, wandered into shallow bays and inlets and would turn up in unlikely spots where residents were never seen. Thinking that these uncommon groups were simply transiting the area, or perhaps were social outcasts of the larger resident pods, they were termed *transients*.

As studies progressed into the 1980s, the true identity of resident and transient populations and their relationship to each other began to be revealed. The most important factor distinguishing residents and transients is their diet – residents specialize on fish prey, particularly salmon, while transients hunt marine mammal prey and appear to shun fish as a food source. These foraging specializations have shaped all aspects of the whales' lifestyles, leading to distinctiveness in behaviour, distribution patterns, social organization, and acoustics. The two are fundamentally different forms of the species that co-exist in social and reproductive isolation along the west coast. This is an extremely unusual situation for any mammal and has raised many unanswered questions about how the two forms evolved.

As our understanding of killer whales in British Columbia grew, so too did the need for a book describing their natural history and for a catalogue of identification photographs so that whale enthusiasts could identify whales themselves. Commercial killer whale watching began in British Columbia in 1980 and quickly became a very popular activity. The first catalogue was published in 1987, co-authored by Mike Bigg, the two of us, and our colleague Ken Balcomb of the Center for Whale Research, Friday Harbor, Washington. This catalogue contained identification photos of all killer whales known at the time in the waters of British Columbia and Washington – 255 residents and 80 transients. It was our plan to update this catalogue every four or five years, but Mike Bigg's death in 1990, at the age of 51, disrupted this schedule. It wasn't until 1994 that the next edition of the catalogue was published, but by this time the number of killer whales known to us had doubled, due in part to growth in the resident pods but also to the discovery of new groups of transients and a previously unknown population we have called *offshores*. A single catalogue with over 700 whale identification photos would have been unwieldy, so we decided to split it into separate volumes. Thus, the 1994 book *Killer Whales: The Natural History and Genealogy of* Orcinus orca *in British Columbia and Washington State* (UBC Press and University of Washington Press) describes all populations of killer whales along the coast but gives special emphasis to residents and contains identification photos of only this population. In the current volume, we focus on the fascinating natural history of the mammal-hunting transients and provide a catalogue of the 219 members of this population that we and our colleagues have identified in the waters of British Columbia, Washington, and southeastern Alaska.

Our current understanding of the identity and biology of transient killer whales is due in large part to the hard work and cooperation of our friends and colleagues along the coast, many of whom made valuable contributions to this catalogue. We thank the following who have graciously shared data on transients collected during the course of their field activities and whose identification photographs are reproduced in this catalogue:

- in British Columbia: Lance Barrett-Lennard, Mike Bigg, Jim Borrowman, Jim Darling, Mike Derry, Brian Falconer, Colin French, Kathy Heise, John McCulloch, Alex Morton, Linda Nichol, Kechura Palm, Rod Palm, Tom Smith, Chris Tulloch, Adam U, and Jane Watson
- in southeastern Alaska: Alex Andrews, Scott Baker, Janet Doherty, Pieter Folkens, Chris Gabriele, Jeff Jacobsen, Dan McSweeney, Dena Matkin, and Jan Straley
- in Washington: Ken Balcomb, John Calambokidis, Bob Devine, David Ellifrit, and Astrid van Ginneken

In addition to those listed above, we are very grateful to all the others who have allowed us to examine their identification photographs or who have helped in other ways in our studies of transients – there are more of them than there are whales in this catalogue. In particular, we thank David Bain, Robin Baird, Kelley Balcomb-Bartok, Nancy Black, David Briggs, Randy Burke, Ginny Collins, Carolyn Cornish, Marilyn Dahlheim, John De Boeck, Volker Deecke, Dori Dick, Fred Felleman, Beverly Ford, Pat Gerlach, Brian Gisborne, Dawn Goley, Karen Hansen, Rick Harbo, Stan Hutchings, John Hyde, Harald Jurk, Brian Kingzett, Ian MacAskie, Bill and Donna Mackay, Rod MacVicar, Beth Mathews, Craig Matkin, Bill McIntyre, Hiromi Naito, Chrys Neville, Erin Nyhan, Peter Olesiuk, Rich Osborne, Bruce Paterson, Derek Rendle, Louis Rzen, Meg Pocklington, Eva Saulitis, Leah Saville, Alisa Schulman-Janiger, Fred Sharpe, Paul Spong, Pam Stacey, Steve Suddes, Helena Symonds, Roy Tanami, Al Whitney, and Steve Wischniowski.

We are grateful to the following organizations for their financial or logistical support of our killer whale studies, and to those researchers whose identification photographs have made this catalogue possible:

Pacific Biological Station, Department of Fisheries and Oceans, Nanaimo, BC
Vancouver Aquarium Marine Science Centre, Vancouver, BC
Marine Mammal Research Unit, University of British Columbia, Vancouver, BC
Stubbs Island Whale Watching, Telegraph Cove, BC
Strawberry Isle Research Society, Tofino, BC
Bluewater Adventures, North Vancouver, BC
Maple Leaf Adventures, Duncan, BC
Glacier Bay National Park, Gustavus, AK
J. Straley Investigations, Sitka, AK
Gwaii Haanas National Park Reserve, Queen Charlotte City, BC
Langara Fishing Lodge, Vancouver, BC
North Gulf Oceanic Society, Homer, AK
Center for Whale Research, Friday Harbor, WA
West Coast Whale Research Foundation, Vancouver, BC
BC Parks, Parksville, BC
Laskeek Bay Conservation Society, Queen Charlotte City, BC
Cascadia Research Collective, Olympia, WA
Sea World, Inc., Orlando, FL
National Marine Mammal Laboratory, Seattle, WA

We are very grateful to Elwood Miles for his long hours in the darkroom printing the fine identification photographs used in our research and reproduced in this book. We also thank George Vaitkunas for the careful conversion of these images into the digital domain and for applying his considerable design skills to this project. Denise Dunn, T. Sinclair, Naomi Stevens, and Peter Thomas kindly allowed the reproduction of their historical photographs of transients. Finally, we very much appreciate the assistance of Lance Barrett-Lennard, Peter Ross, Valerie Shore, Andrew Trites, and Jane Watson, who provided helpful comments on various drafts of this book.

Transient whale T169 spyhopping near Langara Island, BC.
G. Ellis

Natural History
of Transient Killer Whales

Compared to **resident killer whales,** transients are difficult animals to study. They tend to be hard to find and, once found, they are easy to lose. They seem to have no clearly defined patterns of occurrence, unlike resident pods, which congregate predictably in certain locations to intercept migrating salmon. Transients travel in relatively small groups and often hug the shoreline, so they are less conspicuous than the larger resident pods. Their dives are often twice the duration of dives by residents and can occasionally exceed 10 minutes in length. Their movements, especially while foraging, are erratic, with frequent course and speed changes. Close approach by researchers or whale watchers seems to add to this erratic behaviour, likely because the whales attempt to evade the offending boat. Thus, encountering a group of transients is often more a result of good fortune than good tactics, and staying with the group long enough to collect useful identification photographs and behavioural data can be quite challenging.

For these and other reasons, our understanding of the life history and ecology of transient killer whales is far more limited than that of residents. Nonetheless, what we do know is a fascinating study in adaptive specialization, especially when one compares transients to the better-known residents. In the following sections, we describe the latest information available on the feeding habits, social lives, and distribution patterns of these enigmatic mammal-hunters, and how they relate to other killer whale populations along the west coast.

Population Identity, Range, and Size

Transient killer whales are one of at least three distinct and independent forms of the species that share the west coast waters of North America. The known range of transients includes coastal areas from southern California to the Aleutian Islands, Alaska, and about 400 transient whales have been identified to date. Overlapping this range are populations of resident killer whales and offshore killer whales. The resident population ranges from southern Washington north to at least Kodiak Island, Alaska, and comprises about 600 animals. Offshore killer whales are very poorly known from less than 40 encounters to date. Most encounters have taken place around the Queen Charlotte Islands or on shallow banks off the west coast of Vancouver Island, and about 200 whales have been catalogued so far. Some of these same offshore whales have been identified from encounters off central and southern California and southeastern Alaska, but the extent of the population's range is essentially unknown.

Recent DNA studies by our colleague Lance Barrett-Lennard have confirmed earlier suspicions that the three forms of killer whales are genetically discrete, and have identified further genetic distinctiveness within transient and resident populations. Transients are genetically very distant from residents and offshores, likely representing thousands of years of reproductive isolation. Offshores are genetically relatively close to residents, but are nonetheless distinct. Within the transient form, there appear to be at least three genetically distinct populations, and these correspond to patterns of geographic distribution, social association, and acoustic variation.

The transient killer whales that are found along the west coast from southern California to southeastern Alaska form a community of associating individuals and groups. Transients have a very fluid social order, and whales mix with a wide variety of others within the community. Although not every individual has been seen to travel with every other animal in the community, all can be linked together through intermediate associates. All transients in this west coast community that have been recorded acoustically also share a common set of underwater vocal signals.

To the north and west of southeastern Alaska, at least two other transient communities appear to exist. One, known as the "AT1" community, is a small collection of transients that are found mostly within Prince William Sound and in the Kenai Fjords area. Comprising only 22

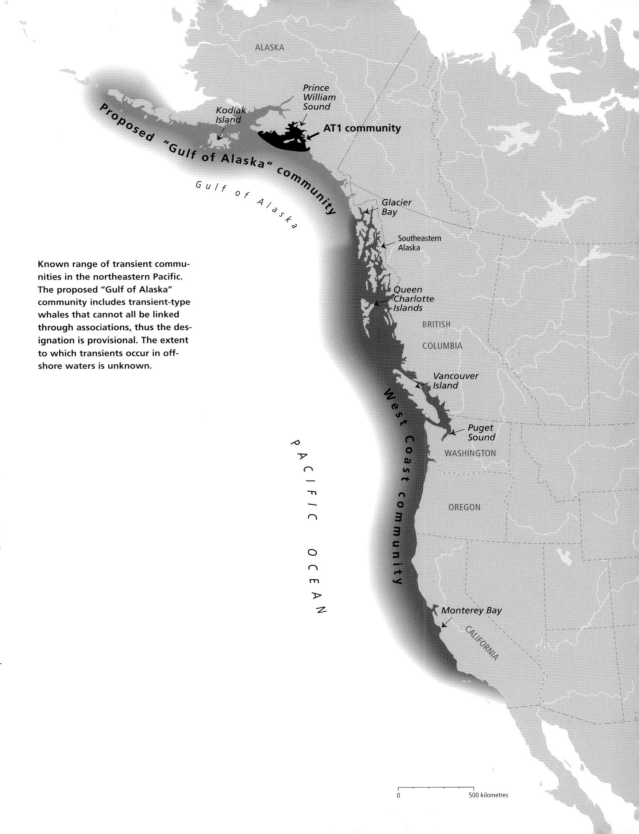

Known range of transient communities in the northeastern Pacific. The proposed "Gulf of Alaska" community includes transient-type whales that cannot all be linked through associations, thus the designation is provisional. The extent to which transients occur in offshore waters is unknown.

whales when first identified in the mid-1980s, this community appears to have declined to about a dozen whales in recent years. Whales identified in the second apparent community are referred to as "Gulf of Alaska" transients, and these are very poorly known. About 60 whales have been identified, although many of these have yet to be linked by association so it remains uncertain whether there is a single community or perhaps more. These Gulf of Alaska transients make occasional forays into Prince William Sound, but they have not been observed to mix with AT1 transients. Although the whales in these two communities feed on marine mammals and have the pointed fin shape generally found among transients (see "Distinguishing Transients and Residents," p. 55), they are genetically and acoustically distinct from each other and from the west coast community. Gulf of Alaska transients have only twice been seen in southeastern Alaska and never in British Columbia or points south.

Transients belonging to the west coast community do not mix evenly up and down the coast. To the south of Washington, about 100 transients have been identified, mostly from the coastal waters of California. Only a few of these Californian transients have been encountered in British Columbia or southeastern Alaska, but when they did so they travelled with local transients and have thus been given "T" designations (see "The Naming System," p. 42). Because transients to the south of Washington rarely mix with those that frequent British Columbia and southeastern Alaska, they can be considered two subcommunities of the overall west coast transient community.

It is likely that additional communities of transient-type killer whales exist in the northeast Pacific Ocean. Further studies are needed to identify and better understand all of these communities, their genetic discreteness, population sizes, feeding habits, and potentially important habitats. In the following sections, we will confine our discussions to information obtained from and relevant to the transient subcommunity found in British Columbia, Washington,

and southeastern Alaska, as these are the best-known transients and the ones for which identification photographs are provided in the catalogue portion of this book. No doubt many aspects of life history, behaviour, and ecology are common to all transient communities, but features unique to each can be expected as well.

Seasonal and Annual Distribution

Transient killer whales can be found in coastal waters of British Columbia, Washington, and southeastern Alaska throughout the year. Most encounters take place during summer and early fall, probably because more observers are out on the water at this time than in winter. Marine-mammal prey species that are favoured by transients are year-round inhabitants of the coast, so food-related seasonality is unlikely to be a major factor in transient movements. Resident whales do show strong seasonal trends in distribution, corresponding to the timing of salmon migrations in summer and fall.

Although transients can be found anywhere along the coast, they are not distributed randomly. As one might expect, the whales tend to be found most frequently in regions where their preferred prey is abundant. Some transient groups have been observed to travel throughout the entire community range, but others have only been seen in particular regions. A few individuals, for example, have only been recorded in the Queen Charlotte Islands, although many others commonly travel between those islands and the mainland coast. When in the Queen Charlottes, visiting whales often travel with the "local" transients. Of the 219 whales in this catalogue, about half have been identified both in southeastern Alaska and in British Columbia, 6 percent have only been seen in southeastern Alaska, and 44 percent have only been encountered in British Columbia and Washington. This would suggest that many transients have preferred home ranges, where they may have local knowledge of prey distribution that would improve hunting success.

Even though a harbour seal haul-out may contain enough prey to feed many transients for a long while, the whales tend not to linger near such locations. Transients hunt with stealth, using the element of surprise to capture unsuspecting seals and other marine mammals. Once potential prey are alert to the presence of the whales, it is no doubt more profitable for the hunters to move on to the next feeding location. Thus, although transients occasionally spend up to a few hours in one spot, they tend to be continuously on the move. A transient group may travel well over 100 kilometres in a single day and can cover a remarkable amount of coastline in a short period. As an example, the young female whale T2B travelled between Frederick Sound, Alaska, and Johnstone Strait, off northeastern Vancouver Island, a straight-line distance of about 800 kilometres, in 11 days. This represents a minimum rate of 75 kilometres per day, but because transients seldom travel long in a straight line, the actual distance travelled by T2B might well have been double that amount.

A puzzling feature of transient distribution is the occasional gap in our sighting records of individuals or groups for periods of many years. Some whales that had been encountered regularly each year have abruptly disappeared for up to a decade, then reappeared with frequent resightings resuming. Where these whales have gone in the intervening years is a mystery, although it is possible that they remained in remote portions of the known community range and eluded detection. These long disappearances make it difficult to calculate mortality rates or current population size for transients, because it is usually uncertain whether a whale has died or is simply on a hiatus from the study area.

Feeding Habits
The single most important factor defining the lifestyle of transient killer whales is their diet. Transients are marine-mammal hunters, and their behaviour, social structure, underwater acoustics, and other aspects of their lives are highly adapted to exploit this prey resource.

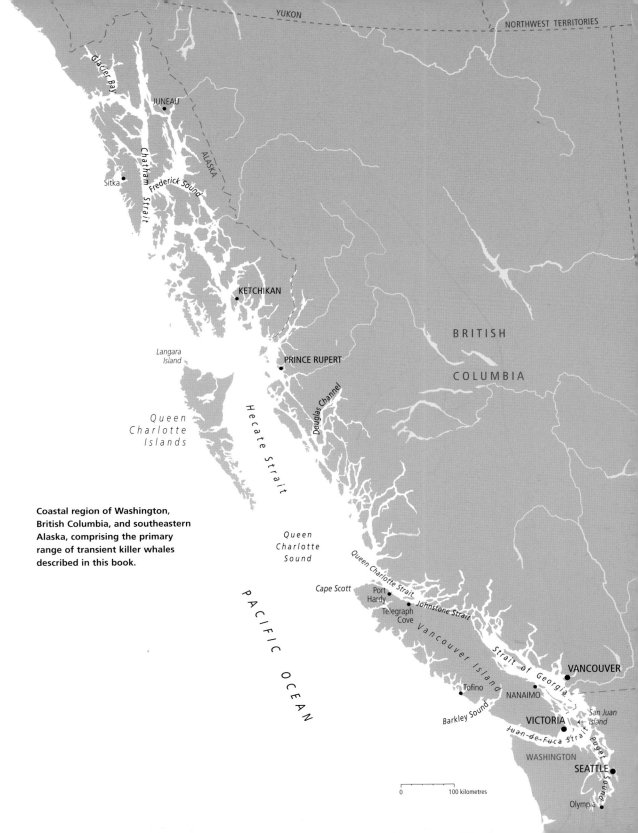

Coastal region of Washington, British Columbia, and southeastern Alaska, comprising the primary range of transient killer whales described in this book.

Top: A group of Steller sea lions showing alarm at the presence of transient whale T12, off Carmanah Point on the west coast of Vancouver Island.

S. Suddes

Bottom: Harbour seals are the most common prey of transients in British Columbia, Washington, and southeastern Alaska.

G. Ellis / Ursus

Our understanding of the diet of transients comes from two sources: observed predatory activities, and food remains in the stomachs of dead, stranded whales. Over the years, we have documented about 200 attacks by transients, the majority of which resulted in the prey being killed. Harbour seals are by far the most common prey item, representing over half of all attacks and kills. Other important prey species include harbour porpoises, Dall's porpoises, and Steller sea lions. We have also documented attacks on California sea lions, Pacific white-sided dolphins, gray whales, minke whales, and river otters, but these prey are less common in the diet of this transient community. Various species of seabirds are also harassed and sometimes killed, but their carcasses are seldom consumed (see "Seabirds," p. 59). So far, we have not observed transients pursuing or taking any fish species.

Stomach contents of stranded whales can reveal much about their diet, but to date we have only been able to examine the stomach of one known transient, the male T15, who we found dead in Boundary Bay, near Vancouver, in 1979. From this whale's stomach we retrieved pieces of skin from an unidentified cetacean, the claws and vibrissae (whiskers) of a northern elephant seal and several harbour seals, the feathers of a white-winged scoter (a common seabird), and a single squid beak. Although it is possible that the whale ate the squid, it is more likely that the beak was in the stomach of the elephant seal, a species that is known to prey regularly on squid. We have also had the opportunity to examine the stomachs of two probable transients who were unknown to us at the time. One large male beached itself on a sandbar while hunting near Tofino on Vancouver Island in 1976. The whale subsequently died and in its stomach were large pieces of two harbour porpoises, the vibrissae of harbour seals and a sea lion, and 394 harbour seal claws, which represent at least 20 seals eaten over an unknown period. The stomach of another probable transient, found dead near Bamfield, Vancouver Island, contained harbour seal remains, feathers of a cormorant, and bits of gray whale baleen.

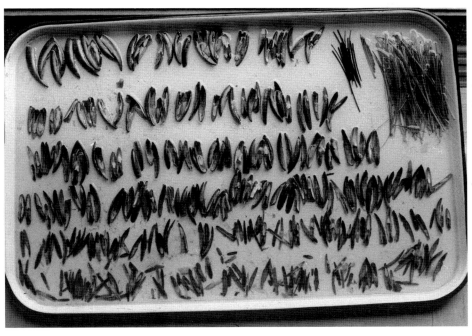

Researcher Jim Darling pouring water on a live-stranded male transient near Tofino, BC, in 1976. The whale subsequently died, and its stomach contents, shown in the adjacent photo, included 394 harbour seal claws, plus vibrissae of harbour seals and a sea lion.

D. Dunn, G. Ellis

An Encounter

The late Mike Bigg was the pioneer of modern killer whale research. Our current understanding of the biology of killer whales is due in large part to his foresight, love for the animals, and cooperative spirit.

The following is an excerpt from our original catalogue of killer whales in British Columbia and Washington State, published in 1987. It was written by the late Michael Bigg to provide the reader with an idea of how we study killer whales and with a sense of the excitement inherent in encounters with transients. We have included it here with only minor updating.

Our introduction to killer whales begins with a recent exciting and important encounter. Details about the encounter are incorporated to illustrate how we study these whales, what we look for, and what type of information we discover.

At noon on 3 December 1986, two of us (Mike Bigg and Graeme Ellis) were working in our office at the Pacific Biological Station, the federal fisheries research institute in Nanaimo, when the phone rang. It was Carole Otley, a regular whale sighter at Dodd Narrows, about 8 miles south of Nanaimo. She had just seen four killer whales heading north into Northumberland Channel, a narrow passage leading toward Nanaimo. The weather and time of day were perfect, so we set out to observe and identify them.

We gathered our equipment, loaded it into our 16-foot boat parked on a trailer behind the office, and drove to a boat-launching ramp a short distance away. It would take about 15 minutes by boat to reach the site. On the way, we discussed the usual concerns. What would be the best strategy to locate the whales? Would this be a new pod? Would it be the resident form or the transient form of killer whale? If we already knew the pod, which was likely to be the case, would any whales be missing (dead) or added (recently born)? Even though we had done this kind of routine many times before, the conversation is still needed to confirm the plan of action, as well as to relieve the tension during this exciting time.

We stopped the boat about a mile from where we estimated the whales would be and scanned the horizon with binoculars, searching for blows or dorsal fins. The whales might have travelled faster than their usual 3-4 knots, and we would not want to miss them. There was a large splash near where the whales should have been, and we accelerated toward it. About 200 yards from the site, we stopped again, put our hydrophone (an underwater microphone) in the water and waited. With the hydrophone, the whales' vocalizations can be heard from several miles away, and from their unique "dialect" we can determine the identity of the pod. We saw and heard nothing for 5 minutes. We were now beginning to think this was a transient pod, which unlike resident pods, tends to be silent and often dives for more than 5 minutes.

The whales began surfacing nearby. There appeared to be four adult females. We recognized only one female, a well-marked transient whale we knew as T16. This indicated that the others would be transients as well, because transients and residents do not travel together. They swam around us rather aimlessly, each going in a different direction, making it difficult to get good photographs for identification. The milling behaviour produced a confusing scene. We repeatedly observed the pod with binoculars, looking for clues to explain their activity. We then spotted an adult male California sea lion lying low in the water nearby. The situation now made sense. The transients had been attacking the sea lion and had been interrupted by our approach. The sea lion was the size of a large black bear, with the strength and teeth to match. He looked alert and uninjured, but lay motionless at the surface. The attack probably had begun only a short time before we arrived.

We sat quietly in the boat and watched. It is not often that we have a chance to witness an attack on a marine mammal. The sea lion slowly made his way toward the shore about 200 yards away. The whales were not concerned by our presence and continued to search for him. Suddenly, when the sea lion was about 100 yards from shore, the whales apparently detected him with their sonar. They dove in unison, accelerating toward him. We saw nothing for about 30 seconds, then the water exploded around him. One after another, the whales charged the sea lion, diving around, under, and over him, smashing him from below and above with their flukes, and ramming him with their heads. Despite this fearsome assault, the sea lion resurfaced every minute or so and continued his slow progress toward shore. The episode lasted about 10 minutes in all. When the sea lion was within about 50 feet of shore, the whales abruptly abandoned him and headed rapidly northward. Perhaps the sea lion was too close to shore for the whales to continue their attack safely.

The sea lion slowly crawled out on the rocks. Surprisingly, he showed no visible injuries, but without a doubt he had had a close call with death. Under other circumstances, the attack could have continued for one or two hours until the sea lion was barely conscious. Then, he would be drowned and eaten. Adult sea lions are tough and dangerous prey for killer whales, and are killed only with considerable effort and caution. His escape meant that another sea lion, seal, or whale would probably be eaten later in the day, as transients specialize in hunting marine mammals.

We followed the whales north for about an hour. They eventually slowed and swam in a tightly packed group, which provided an ideal opportunity for us to take photographs and record behaviour and sounds. We identified another adult female as T17 (see p. 50), a transient that had been a constant companion of T16 for at least the past 12 years. Both are probably old females that are past their reproductive age. The identity of the other two whales would be established when their photographs were examined back at the lab. They turned out to be T26 and T27 (see p. 52), another pair of apparently old and non-reproductive females, which we last photographed during March 1976 in southern Puget Sound. They had been captured for the oceanarium Sea World, along with four other transients (T46, T47, T13, and T14) (see pp. 48 and 56, and "Capture and Radio-Tagging of T13 and T14," p. 49). The capture caused a public outcry and eventually resulted in the release of all six whales. These were the last killer whales to be caught in Washington for aquaria. Where T16 and T17 had spent the past 11 years is unknown, but it is not unusual for transients to disappear from this region for years at a time.

Apart from the attack on the sea lion, the encounter was typical of the opportunities we have for gathering data on killer whales.

Steller sea lion being rammed by transient T7A in Blackfish Sound, BC. The attack continued for over one hour before the sea lion was finally killed and eaten.
J. Borrowman

Top: Hunting transient attempting to catch a Dall's porpoise, seen in the small splash ahead of the whale, near Chatham Point, Vancouver Island.

L. Barrett-Lennard

Bottom: Portion of the throat area of a minke whale taken by killer whales, near Port Hardy, BC.

J. Ford / Ursus

Together, our field observations and the stomach contents data argue strongly that transients are hunters of marine mammals and, to a lesser extent, seabirds, but are not interested in fish as a food resource. Their interest in warm-blooded prey even extends to terrestrial mammals such as deer, which frequently swim between islands along the inside passage (see "Land Mammals As Transient Prey," p. 29). Transient prey preferences are in striking contrast to the diet of resident killer whales, which appear to feed exclusively on fish, especially salmon and squid. Residents have been seen to harass porpoises and harbour seals occasionally, but there is no evidence that these animals were killed and eaten. We cannot discount the possibility that transients do take fish from time to time, and residents eat an occasional marine mammal, but such events must be quite uncommon. Indeed, many of the behavioural traits of transients and residents seem to be adaptations for exploiting their respective favoured prey and would make them inefficient predators of other types of prey species. We have little information on the diet of offshore killer whales, but we suspect that they are primarily fish or squid feeders.

Social Structure

Transients tend to travel in small groups of two to six, or occasionally alone. Eighty percent of our encounters with transients involve groups of six or fewer. Temporary groupings of over 12 transients have been documented, but these are quite unusual. Like resident killer whales, the basic social unit of transient whales is the maternal group, which comprises a mother and her offspring. However, there are several important differences between the social structures of residents and transients. In residents, there is no dispersal of individuals from the maternal group, so an animal born to a group stays with it for life. For this reason, maternal groups can grow to contain a mother and up to five or so offspring. Furthermore, because killer whales are long-lived, female offspring in the group can themselves have calves while their mother is still reproductively active, so that three or, in rare cases, four generations of whales can exist at a time to form a large *matrilineal* group. A typical resident pod consists of one to several related matrilineal groups; thus they often contain 15 to 30 or more whales.

In transients, a whale born to a group does not necessarily stay with that group for life. Whales of both sexes may leave their mother, either as a juvenile or adult, to travel alone or with a variety of transient associates. This dispersal is not always permanent, as a whale may occasionally be seen back with its natal, or birth, group. However, due to the lack of long-term stability in transient maternal groups, they tend not to reach the size of those in resident societies (a good example of the fluidity of transient society is the T2 lineage, described on pp. 20-21). Also, maternal groups travel alone for the majority of time, and if they choose to associate with other whales, it is typically for a short term. As a result, transient society tends to be far more dynamic than that of residents, and the typical group size is much smaller. As these differences have become more clear to us over the years, we have chosen not to refer to transient groups as "pods," preferring to restrict that term to the highly structured and stable social units defined for residents.

The different social structures of transients and residents are tied closely to their feeding specializations. Transients primarily hunt relatively small marine mammals using a "sneak attack" tactic, where the group maintains underwater silence to avoid detection by their intended prey. Small groups can easily find and subdue such prey, and a harbour seal or porpoise provides enough food for sharing among group members. If transients foraged in larger groups, vocal signalling might be necessary to coordinate its members, and this would compromise the "element of surprise" that may be important for hunting success. Resident whales, on the other hand, forage for schools of fish that often have a patchy distribution. Large resident groups, which fan out while foraging, may be more successful in locating fish schools than would small groups or individuals.

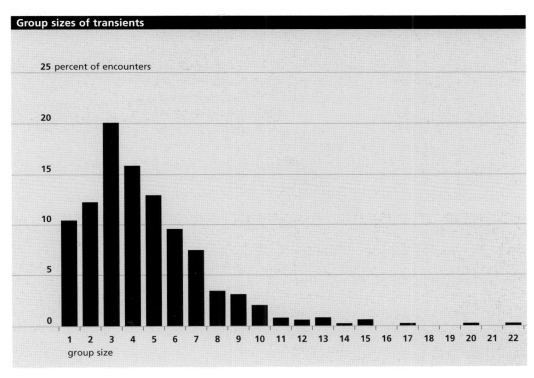

Group sizes of transients

25 percent of encounters

group size

Group sizes of transients tend to be relatively small. The most common group size is three whales, and the maximum recorded was 22.

Alice, Charlie Chin, and Chimo: The Story of the T2 Lineage

By far the best-known lineage of transients is that of the female T2, her ancestors, and her descendants. It is a story of historical interest, as well as being an excellent example of the fluidity of transient society. The story begins in the mid-1940s, when a white killer whale began to be reported regularly around Vancouver Island and the south coast of mainland British Columbia. These sightings were compiled by the late Clifford Carl, of the BC Provincial Museum, Victoria, BC, who named the whale Alice. She was usually reported in the company of two to four normally coloured whales. Although details are sketchy, it appears that around 1950 another white whale was born to this group, and the original Alice disappeared shortly thereafter. During the remainder of the 1950s, only a single white whale was reported. In January 1958, this group of whales

Female transient T3 with unidentified white whale off Victoria, BC, in January 1958.
T. Sinclair

was photographed by onlookers close to shore in Victoria. These photos revealed a subadult white whale and two other normally coloured whales that would later prove to be individually identifiable.

There are no records of Alice's group in the 1960s, but in 1970 a group of five whales, including a white juvenile, was netted at Pedder Bay, near Victoria. At the time, killer whales in the area were still being live-captured for display in oceanaria. This group included an adult female, identified as T2, her presumed subadult son T1, an adult female T3, her presumed daughter T4, who was white, and another young female T5. The male, T1, had an unusual facial deformity and became known as Charlie Chin, the white whale came to be known as Chimo, and T5 was named Nootka.

Interestingly, T2 and T3 proved to be the two females in the 1958 photographs, but it was a different white whale in those early photos. It is likely that this white whale, who was probably the offspring of T3, died after 1958, and around 1965, T3 gave birth to Chimo. Also during the 1960s, T2 appears to have given birth to T1 around 1960, and possibly to T5 around 1963.

Shortly after the capture in 1970, Chimo (T4) and Nootka (T5) were moved to an aquarium in Victoria. Chimo subsequently died of an infection in 1972 and was found to have a rare genetic disorder known as Chediak-Higashi syndrome. This inherited syndrome, which is also known in humans, results in partial albinism, a high susceptibility to infection, and a below-average life expectancy. Nootka was subsequently moved to aquaria in Ontario, California, and Texas, before finally ending up at Sea World, San Diego, where she died in 1990.

The remaining three whales from the group were held in a sea pen at Pedder Bay for several months. For many weeks, the whales refused all fish offered

to them, no doubt because of the strong mammal-eating tradition common to all transients. After 75 days of starvation, T3 died of apparent malnutrition. At last, on day 79, T2 and Charlie Chin started eating salmon and herring. They lived on this unfamiliar diet for another four and a half months until finally they were released by unknown persons, who threw weights over the floating nets one night to make an escape route for the whales.

After release, T1 and T2 returned to a typical transient lifestyle, hunting harbour seals and other marine mammals. T2 gave birth to T2A around 1972, and the trio was encountered many times around southern Vancouver Island over the next six years. Then, in late 1978 or early 1979, T2 gave birth to another calf, T2B, and around the same time T2A disappeared. The group continued to be among the most commonly encountered transients during the late 1970s and early 1980s, and certainly among the most stable. The three were always seen together and, unlike most transients, were never observed to associate with others in their community.

In 1986, a number of interesting developments took place in the T2 story. First, Charlie Chin (T1) began to wander away from the group for the first time. Although he occasionally turned up back with T2 and T2B, he often was encountered alone in locations as distant as the Queen Charlotte Islands. In the fall of 1986, we encountered T2's son T2A, who had disappeared in 1978. We found him alone, chasing seabirds off northern Vancouver Island. Where he had been for those eight years remains a mystery. Also in 1986, T2 and T2B were seen travelling with other transients, another "first" for the group.

Over the next few years, Charlie Chin continued to travel with T2 and T2B on a periodic basis. T2A was encountered several more times, then was seen for the last time in Glacier Bay, southeastern Alaska, in 1988. Whether he is dead or has left the region is unknown. In the winter of 1988-89, T2 had a new calf, T2C, and the four whales, T1, T2, T2B, and T2C, became a fairly stable unit, mixing occasionally with other transients. Then, early in 1992, T2B began to spend most of her time apart from her mother's group, and Charlie Chin disappeared. As with T2A, we do not know whether he has dispersed from the area or is dead.

During the past decade, T2B has continued to associate with a variety of different transients, especially the T21 and T88 groups. Only occasionally is she seen back with her mother and younger sibling. So far, T2C has not been seen far from her mother's side. In the future, the T2 lineage will no doubt continue to yield new insights into the intriguing social dynamics of transients, especially if T2B and T2C have calves of their own.

Transient T1, known as Charlie Chin, with his presumed mother, T2, in a net-pen near Victoria, BC, 1970.
N. Stevens

The white whale, T4, known as Chimo, swimming alongside her presumed mother, T3, in a net-pen near Victoria, BC, 1970.
P. Thomas

Because most fish species are insensitive to the frequencies used by killer whales for communication and echolocation, resident group activities can be coordinated through vocal signalling without affecting the catchability of their prey.

Vocal Behaviour and Dialects

As mentioned above, transients are very quiet whales compared to residents. But transients do vocalize in certain situations, and the structure and function of their acoustic signals are similar to those used by residents.

The underwater sounds produced by killer whales are of three basic types: clicks, burst-pulsed signals, and whistles. Clicks are used for echolocation, the whales' primary means of navigating and discriminating objects under water. Clicks are typically emitted in long series, or click trains, with the timing of click repetition corresponding roughly to the distance of the objects being "pinged" by their sonar. Transients use echolocation far less often than residents, most likely because of their sneak-attack hunting strategy (see "Silence of the Transients," p. 78). Whistles and burst-pulsed sounds are used primarily as communication signals within and between groups. These are complex and varied sounds, usually less than two seconds in duration, that can have shrill, scream-like qualities. Most of the social signals used by killer whales for maintaining contact while the whales are out of sight of each other are quite stereotyped and distinctive in structure. Each individual or group of whales produces a certain number and type of these repetitive *discrete calls*.

In resident killer whales, each pod has a repertoire of between 7 and 17 discrete calls that can vary considerably from group to group. These consistent variations form the group's *dialect*, and each pod can be identified acoustically using this dialect. Although the actual mechanism of call acquisition in residents is unknown, it is probable that the dialect is passed down from generation to generation by vocal learning, where calves mimic their mothers and close kin to learn the distinctive call repertoire of their group.

Errors in call learning lead to drift in dialects of pods that were historically closely related. It is likely that dialects are important to the whales as acoustic indicators of group identity and membership, and serve to help maintain the stability and cohesion of the pod.

A very different dialect system exists within the transient community. The discrete call repertoire of transients is smaller than residents, with only four to six calls, none of which is used by resident whales. The striking variations seen in dialects of resident pods are not present among transient groups. Every transient group shares at least two discrete calls, and most have all calls in common. However, some regional differences in the transient dialect exist. Transients in California produce a few call types and variations that are not heard in British Columbia, and some groups that are found mostly in southeastern Alaska also produce a call that is not heard elsewhere. As mentioned previously, calls used by the "AT1" and "Gulf of Alaska" transient communities differ from those heard along the mainland west coast.

The lack of a well-developed dialect system in transients reflects and perhaps results from the fluidity of their social structure. Because individuals frequently disperse from their natal group and join others, there is little opportunity for group-specific dialects to evolve in a lineage, and likely there is little need for them. However, the distinctive and widespread calls of transients may serve the whales as reliable indicators of community membership and may play a role in maintaining the identity and cohesion of transient society.

Population Parameters

Most of what we know about vital life history parameters in the species comes from 25 years of detailed chronicling of demographic events in the resident population in British Columbia and Washington. Because of the unusually stable pod structure of residents, and because most pods can be censused by photo-identification each year, it has been possible to determine with good precision the mortality rates of various age classes – when females have their first and subsequent calves, what calf survival rates are, and so on. However, such data are extremely difficult to obtain for transients. Because transients range widely and are unpredictable in their movements, years can pass between sightings of some groups. As a result, it is often not possible to know whether females have had and lost calves between encounters, nor can the year of birth be determined accurately for surviving calves. Similarly, because individuals disperse from their mother's group, it is not possible to know whether an animal that has disappeared is dead, or is alive and well in some other part of the community range. Some whales have disappeared for over 10 years between encounters. Thus, the following information on population parameters is based on residents, but is likely applicable to transients as well.

Female killer whales typically give birth for the first time at 11 to 15 years of age. There are only two female transients for which we have a known age at first reproduction, and these took place at ages 12 and 13 years. The gestation period, determined from studies of whales in aquaria, is 16 to 17 months, and only a single calf is born at a time (earlier reports of twins in residents were found to be erroneous). Calves are about 2.5 metres in length at birth and weigh about 200 kilograms. They nurse for at least one year, but probably start taking solid food from their mothers at six months or so. Weaning may be a protracted procedure in killer whales, and young may continue occasional nursing for social reasons for a number of years. The mortality rate of resident calves is quite high, with an estimated 40 percent dying in their first year. Whether survival of calves is as poor in transients is not known, but similar rates can be expected. The shortest interval between successful calving in killer whales is three years, and a female can give birth regularly until age 40 or so, accumulating up to four to six surviving offspring in the process. Post-reproductive females may live for an additional 25 years or more, although the average lifespan for females is about 50 years.

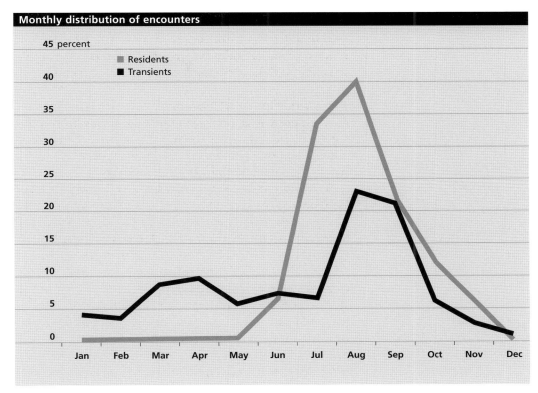

Monthly distribution of encounters

This graph shows the proportion of encounters with residents and transients in waters off northeastern Vancouver Island by month. Residents tend to have a strong seasonal peak in encounters during June through October. Transients are less distinctly seasonal, with many encounters taking place during winter and spring.

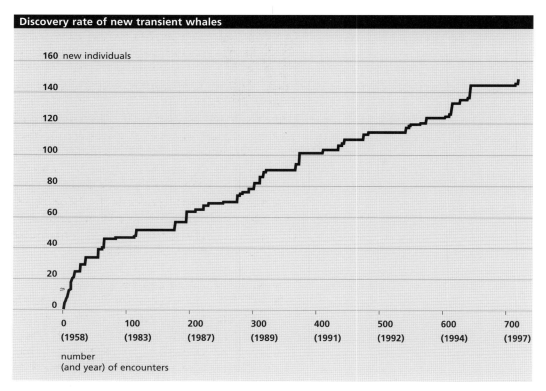

Discovery rate of new transient whales

160 new individuals

140

120

100

80

60

40

20

0

| 0 | 100 | 200 | 300 | 400 | 500 | 600 | 700 |
| (1958) | (1983) | (1987) | (1989) | (1991) | (1992) | (1994) | (1997) |

number
(and year) of encounters

This graph shows the rate of discovery of new transient whales in British Columbian waters over the course of our study. The vertical axis represents the cumulative number of individuals identified in the population, excluding calves born to known whales during the study. The total number of encounters in which whales were identified is indicated on the horizontal axis, beginning with the first encounter in 1958 and ending with over 700 encounters in 1997. The steeper the curve, the greater is the rate at which new individuals were identified. Various plateaus in the graph indicate periods in which no new whales were found. The graph indicates that the rate at which new transients are being discovered in recent years may be slowing, but nonetheless some new animals are still being discovered in most years.

The life expectancy of males is shorter than females, averaging about 30 years. Some males, however, can live substantially longer. One transient male, T105, was photographed as a mature bull in 1974, indicating that he is now at least 45 years old. Males begin maturing at 12 to 14 years of age, revealed by a sudden growth spurt in their dorsal fin. They grow rapidly, attaining physical maturity at about 20 years. Males reach about 8 to 9 metres in length and a weight of 9 or 10 metric tonnes. Mature females are smaller, measuring 7 to 8 metres in length and weighing 7 to 8 metric tonnes.

We have found that the resident population in British Columbia and Washington has expanded at annual rates of up to 2 to 3 percent from the mid-1970s to the mid-1990s, but this growth may now be slowing. Unfortunately, for the reasons outlined above, it is not possible to determine trends in population size for transients. The 219 whales listed in this catalogue represent an increase of 275 percent over the 80 whales listed in our 1987 catalogue, but this should not be interpreted as growth in the overall population. The increase can mostly be attributed to expansion of our study area to include the waters of the Queen Charlotte Islands and southeastern Alaska over the past decade, continued discovery of new transient groups in British Columbia, and increased observer effort generally. Because of the long periods between resightings of some animals, a few individuals in this catalogue may actually be dead. Thus, the actual current population size of transients, and whether it is increasing or decreasing, remains uncertain.

Watching Transient Killer Whales

Watching transients can be an exercise in extremes. At times, it can be rather tedious. Watching two or three whales moving at a steady pace and surfacing at regular intervals hour after hour without displaying any other behaviours can bore even enthusiastic first-time whale watchers. Yet suddenly, without warning, those same whales can burst into a spectacular 20-knot chase of a Dall's porpoise that they have detected ahead of them, leaping high into the air in an attempt to ram or jump on their swift prey. At such times, transients can be the most exciting of any whale species. In the following section, we introduce you to some of the activities and behaviours of transients and suggest how to watch transients in ways that minimize potential disturbance.

Transient Activities and Behaviours

The activities of transient killer whale groups, like those of residents, are of four general types: *foraging, travelling, resting,* and *socializing.* In residents, these categories are not exclusive – for example, some pod members may engage in socializing activities while others are resting or foraging. In smaller transient groups, however, all members tend to be in the same activity state at the same time.

Foraging. When one first encounters a group of transients, chances are the whales will be on the hunt for marine mammals. Overall, transients spend as much as 90 percent of daylight hours foraging for food, which is considerably greater than the time (60-65 percent) that residents devote to foraging. Transients hunt in two general ways: *nearshore foraging* and *open-water foraging.* When nearshore foraging, the whales hug the shoreline and swim relatively close together. Group members often surface and dive at the same time, although sometimes individuals will be out of sync with the rest of the group. Foraging groups follow the shoreline contour closely, crossing open water only to move to the other side of a channel or to patrol a reef area that

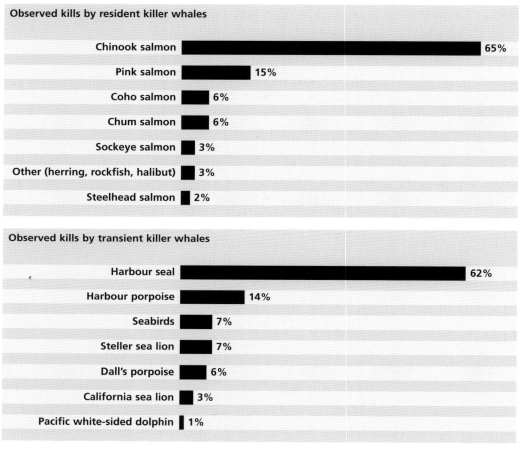

Observed kills by resident killer whales

Prey	Percentage
Chinook salmon	65%
Pink salmon	15%
Coho salmon	6%
Chum salmon	6%
Sockeye salmon	3%
Other (herring, rockfish, halibut)	3%
Steelhead salmon	2%

Observed kills by transient killer whales

Prey	Percentage
Harbour seal	62%
Harbour porpoise	14%
Seabirds	7%
Steller sea lion	7%
Dall's porpoise	6%
California sea lion	3%
Pacific white-sided dolphin	1%

These diagrams illustrate the radically different diets of residents and transients, as determined by kills we have observed or documented over the past 25 years. Residents have not been seen killing and eating any marine mammal but rather are clearly focused on salmon as their primary prey. Transients, on the other hand, specialize on marine mammals and have not been observed to eat any fish.

may contain prey. Along exposed, rocky coastlines, the whales frequently disappear into the white water of breaking surf as they patrol the near shore. Transients seem often to have considerable local knowledge of good hunting sites and will change course to head directly to a harbour seal haul-out while still a considerable distance away.

When open-water foraging, transients spread out, often in a rough line abreast and swim steadily in a consistent direction. As with nearshore foraging, long dives of seven to ten minutes are separated by three or four short, shallow dives, each less than a minute long. This pattern can continue for hours, broken only if prey is located and pursued. Open-water foraging seems to be a tactic for hunting Dall's or harbour porpoises, although other species of prey may be taken as well. Nearshore foraging, however, is primarily a technique for hunting harbour seals.

While foraging, transients are typically intent on finding food and exhibit little variety in their behaviours. Rarely do they interact socially with others in their group or display any aerial behaviours such as breaching or spyhopping. Under water, the whales maintain virtual silence, seldom calling or using echolocation (see "Silence of the Transients," p. 78). These traits all reflect the hunting tactic used by transients – that of stealthy foraging and sneak attacks. Unsuspecting prey seems to be detected visually at close range or by passive listening at greater distances for underwater vocalizations or hydrodynamic swimming sounds generated by the marine mammals. Once prey is detected at a suitable range, the transients attack.

Depending on the type of prey involved, attacks by transients can be over in seconds or continue for hours. Harbour seals are relatively easy prey for transients, especially seal pups during summer and fall. Ninety percent of the harbour seal attacks we have documented ended with the animal being killed and eaten, and in the remaining cases the whales were probably successful but the seal simply disappeared and a kill could not be confirmed. The whales either chase and grasp harbour seals directly in their mouths, or strike it with their tails a few times to immobilize the animal before tearing it up and consuming it. The prey is often shared among group members.

Attacks on Steller or California sea lions are less common and involve greater time, effort, and risk for the transients than attacks on harbour seals. Steller sea lions can weigh up to 1,000 kilograms and can mount a dangerous defense with their large canine teeth. As a result, sea lions are probably only taken on if conditions are right. On average, sea lions are attacked by larger groups of transients than groups hunting harbour seals (mean transient group sizes of 5.4 versus 3.75). If the whales encounter a sea lion swimming far from shore, they will surround the animal to prevent it from escaping to land, then take repeated turns rushing in and striking it with their tail flukes or ramming it with their heads. This may continue for one or two hours, until the sea lion is badly debilitated and weakened sufficiently for the whales to seize and drown it under water. Once killed, the sea lion is ripped apart and shared among group members. In one case, the whales were still carrying around large chunks of sea lion flesh over an hour after the animal was killed. Sea lion attacks are often unsuccessful, however. In about half of the cases we studied, the sea lions managed to escape or the whales abandoned the attack.

About one-quarter of transient attacks we have documented have involved small cetaceans – harbour porpoises, Dall's porpoises, and Pacific white-sided dolphins. As with attacks on sea lions, transients are usually in larger groups when hunting porpoises or dolphins, but probably for a different reason. Although porpoises and dolphins are not dangerous or difficult to subdue, they can be very swift and evasive in open water. It seems that several whales (five on average), working in close cooperation, are often needed to catch them. In such cases, one whale may start pursuing a porpoise but others soon join in, either taking turns in the chase or cutting off avenues of escape. Once the porpoise begins to tire and slow down, the whales attempt to kill the animal by jumping onto it from above or ramming it from

below. These high-speed chases are typical of attacks on Dall's porpoises, which are speedier than the smaller harbour porpoises. Indeed, Dall's porpoises are considered to be one of the fastest swimming cetaceans, perhaps as an adaptation for escaping killer whale predation. In more than half of Dall's porpoise attacks we have observed, the intended prey got away.

Transients seem to use a different tactic when hunting Pacific white-sided dolphins, which travel in much larger groups than either of the two porpoise species. In attacks on these dolphins, the whales seem to try to split a small group or individual away from the larger school, which may number several hundred, then drive and corral them into a shallow bay or inlet. There, the dolphins become trapped against the shore and are easily captured in the ensuing panic. On several occasions in the last few years, such drive hunts have resulted in a number of dolphins becoming stranded on shore and dying.

Attacks by transients on larger whales are quite rare, at least in British Columbian and southeastern Alaskan waters. On two documented occasions, gray whale calves migrating with their mothers along the west coast of Vancouver Island have been attacked, although no kills were confirmed (see "Large Whales As Transient Prey," p. 69). Transients in Monterey Bay, California, often prey on the vulnerable calves during the spring migration. We recently watched a group of nine transients pursue a minke whale over a distance of 10 kilometres at speeds of up to 13 knots – and the minke got away. Not all minkes are so lucky, however. In the mid-1960s, a group of seven killer whales, almost certainly transients, were seen to kill a minke whale in Barkley Sound on the west coast of Vancouver Island. After the killer whales had left the scene, the minke's carcass was examined and found to have had its tongue and flesh of the lower jaw removed, and its skin was neatly ripped off, giving the minke the appearance of a "freshly peeled orange." Although certain transients may have prey preferences within their mammalian diet, there is no evidence that individuals or groups specialize on particular types, such as seals or porpoises. Transients seen foraging near shore for harbour seals one day are just as likely to be found hunting porpoises in a larger group the next. The whales seem adaptable and flexible enough to exploit whatever prey is available, so long as it is warm-blooded. They have even been seen hunting terrestrial prey on rare occasions (see opposite page).

Travelling. Although it is often difficult to be sure when transients are interested in food or not, there are occasions when the whales seem to be simply transiting the area without foraging. We categorize such activity as *travelling*. When travelling, the whales tend to group closely together and surface synchronously, maintaining a steady course. This activity is not very common, amounting to only a small percentage of the total observation time.

Resting. Transients are considered to be resting when the group slows considerably or stops, and individuals group together and either float quietly at the surface or make long dives with little or no forward movement. Surfacings tend to be closely coordinated. The whales are completely silent under water while resting. Resting is rarely seen in transients, representing less than 3 percent of their overall activity budget, compared to 10 to 15 percent for residents.

Socializing. Socializing involves a wide range of interactions between individuals as well as behavioural displays. Whales may exhibit much splashing and chasing, with frequent physical contact between individuals. Spyhops, breaches, and flipper slaps are also common. Socializing may have a variety of functions depending on the context. Some interactions might involve courtship or mating, others may be more aggressive in nature, while those among young whales probably represent play. Although transients are usually very quiet under water, they often emit a tremendous variety of whistles and calls while socializing. As with resting,

socializing is seen less frequently among transients than residents, and most often after a successful hunt.

Where to Find Transients

Transients can be found in all coastal waters of British Columbia, Washington, or southeastern Alaska, but there is no location where sightings are guaranteed. On the other hand, there is really nowhere on the west coast where one can be guaranteed of *not* sighting a transient group. Because their mammalian prey is found coastwide throughout the year, so too are transients. Unlike resident killer whales, which congregate at certain locations to prey on seasonally abundant salmon, transients move widely and unpredictably. They are seen frequently along the wild exposed coasts of Vancouver Island and the Queen Charlotte Islands, but they also roam far into deep mainland fjords.

Transients can be observed from vessels or from shore. Passengers on ferries or cruise ships plying the inside passage may spot groups of transients, but such encounters tend to be limited to one or two surfacings before the ship has passed. Hikers in Pacific Rim National Park on Vancouver Island often glimpse transients foraging along the surf line. Because of the sporadic occurrence of transients, they tend not to be the target species of commercial whale-watch operators. But when whale-watch vessels happen upon a group of transients, the mammal hunters quickly become the focus of interest. Whale-watching areas where transients are encountered frequently include southern and northern Vancouver Island, Clayoquot Sound on the west coast of Vancouver Island, the Gwaii Haanas area of the Queen Charlotte Islands, and Frederick Sound in southeastern Alaska. The summer core areas of resident killer whales, such as Johnstone Strait off northeast Vancouver Island and Haro Strait off southeastern Vancouver Island, are not the best locations for transient watching, perhaps because transients tend to avoid these larger resident pods (see "Residents vs. Transients," p. 83).

Land Mammals As Transient Prey

Although the primary prey of transient killer whales are marine mammals, the whales' interest extends to other warm-blooded animals, including marine birds (see "Seabirds," p. 59) and even terrestrial mammals. Our first record of land mammal predation dates from June 1961, when Canadian fishery officers observed killer whales feeding on a

Deer are common along shorelines of British Columbia and southeastern Alaska and frequenty swim across channels where they occasionally fall prey to transient killer whales.

J. Ford / Ursus

deer carcass in Jackson Pass on the central coast of British Columbia. Deer frequently swim from island to island along the inside passages, and it is probable that this one fell victim to a foraging group of transients. More recently, off the east coast of Vancouver Island, several killer whales were observed circling a small rock on which two deer had taken refuge. On another occasion, a lighthouse keeper assisted an exhausted deer out of the water as it was being pursued by killer whales. In these cases, there has been no photographic confirmation that transients were involved, but it seems almost certainly the case.

Other land mammals are also of interest to transients on occasion. Some years ago, a killer whale was observed to surge part way onto shore in an apparent attempt to attack a dog that was barking loudly at the passing group. We have also heard of a similar case involving a black bear walking near the shallows. In 1989, a dead killer whale stranded on a beach in the Queen Charlotte Islands was found to have pig's teeth in its throat. Although it is conceivable that the whale had actually taken the pig – there was a small pig farm nearby – there is reason to believe that this actually was a hoax and that a prankster placed the teeth in the dead whale's throat.

One of the most surprising attacks on a terrestrial mammal took place in 1993 in Icy Strait, southeastern Alaska. Two fisherman observed a group of three or four killer whales attack and kill one of a pair of moose that were swimming across the channel. The other moose managed to escape the attack but later became tangled in a kelp bed and drowned.

If transients so eagerly attack non-marine mammals, might they also be so inclined should they encounter a vulnerable human swimmer? There are no authenticated cases of wild killer whales attacking and killing a human, although in 1972 a surfer in California was apparently bitten and released by a killer whale. Scuba divers sometimes encounter transients, but no interactions have yet been documented. Divers in this region typically wear thick suits made of neoprene rubber, which contains acoustically reflective nitrogen bubbles. Thus, if a transient tries to inspect a diver with echolocation, its unlikely to get a typical mammalian echo. Although scuba divers may not appear appetizing to transients, this may not be the case for swimmers, so it is advisable to leave the water should transients appear in the vicinity.

Watching Transients without Disturbing Them

Observing wild killer whales is a wonderful experience, but care must be taken so that the whales are not disturbed or their activities disrupted. This is especially true for transients, which in certain cases may be more vulnerable to disturbance than resident whales. Transients usually travel in much smaller groups than residents, so whale-watch boats can easily outnumber the whales in congested areas. Because transients dive for periods of 5 to 10 minutes, and since they may travel considerable distances and change direction under water, it is difficult to predict where the whales will next surface. Thus, following slowly parallel to the whales, as can usually be done with residents, is difficult when watching transients. It is important to resist the temptation to rush from one surfacing spot to the next, as this creates considerable noise and disturbance for the whales. Instead, follow the whale-watching guidelines given on the opposite page and be prepared to watch transients through binoculars.

We suspect that transients may be more susceptible than residents to disturbance from vessels through the masking effects of engine noise. Acoustical studies have shown that transients hunt very quietly, no doubt to prevent detection by their mammalian prey, which have good underwater hearing. This quietness also extends to echolocation clicks, which are used commonly by residents hunting fish but infrequently and in modified form by transients (see "Silence of the Transients," p. 78). Instead of using echolocation to find prey, we believe that transients often hunt with "passive sonar," which simply involves listening to and homing in on the sounds produced by their prey. These sounds might include the splashes of a harbour seal in the shallows, the puffing of a surfacing porpoise, or the whistles and clicks of dolphins. Because many of these sounds may be faint, the whales probably need a quiet ambient noise background in order to detect and locate them. Boats travelling nearby may well mask these sounds and interfere with the whales' hunting. On several occasions we have followed transients foraging unsuccessfully for several hours while we took identification photographs, only to have the whales make a kill within moments of shutting off our boat's motor. Thus, it is important to maintain a minimum distance of 100 metres from transients and to limit your whale-watching to reasonable periods of time. Watching transients quietly at a distance may well yield a more rewarding experience than closely following the whales, as predation and other behaviours are more likely to be witnessed.

Whale-Watching Guidelines:
Giving Transients Space and Quiet

Whale watching is becoming an increasingly popular recreational and commercial activity in coastal British Columbia, Washington, and southeastern Alaska. As the number of boats following whales increases, so too does the potential for causing serious disturbance to the animals. Recent studies of interactions between whale watchers and resident killer whales off northeastern Vancouver Island have shown significant effects of boats on the whales' swimming and diving behaviour. Whether these effects result in long-term impacts on resident whales is uncertain, but it is best to exercise caution.

Whale watching may well have a greater potential to cause negative impacts on transients than on residents. Transients tend to be rather erratic in their swimming patterns and may cover long distances under water during their 5 to 10 minute dives, so the location of surfacings can be quite unpredictable. In order to maintain a good viewing range to the whales, boaters sometimes accelerate quickly to catch up to surfacing whales before they go under on another long dive. This creates much more noise under water than does a boat cruising steadily at whale speed, and the

sudden rush often startles the whales, causing them to abbreviate their surfacing and become evasive. Because transients usually travel in small groups, the attention of many boats can be simultaneously focused on only a few whales. Also, unlike residents, transients appear to use quiet, unobtrusive echolocation and passive listening to locate prey. Noise created by boats following the whales closely may mask these sounds and decrease the whales' hunting success.

Another good reason to give hunting transients a lot of space is the potential for whale-watch boats to serve as haul-out platforms for fleeing prey. On several occasions in both British Columbia and Alaska, terrified harbour seals and Steller sea lions have climbed aboard nearby boats in their attempt to escape from attacking transients. Once on board, the animals are reluctant to leave and could be quite dangerous to the boat's human passengers.

By following the whale-watching guidelines below, boaters can enjoy viewing transients while minimizing disturbance.

1 From a distance, determine the travel direction and diving sequence of the whales.

2 Approach whales gradually from the side, not from the front or the rear. Approach and depart slowly, avoiding sudden changes in speed or direction. Do not "leapfrog" ahead of the whales.

3 Maintain low speeds and constant direction if travelling parallel to whales. When whales are travelling close to shore, avoid crowding them near shore or coming between the whales and shore.

Continued on next page

Boaters viewing transients off northeastern Vancouver Island. Close and repeated approaches by vessels may disrupt behaviour and hunting success of transients.
J. Ford / Ursus

4 Approach no closer than 100 metres and shift your motor into neutral or idle. If possible, shut down your motor. Start your motor and get under way only if the whales are more than 100 metres from your vessel. Leave the area slowly, gradually accelerating when more than 300 metres from the whales.

5 Limit the time spent with any group of whales to less than 30 minutes when within 100 to 200 metres of whales.

6 Be considerate of other whale watchers so that all have a chance to view without disturbance. If several boats are following one group of whales, wait until one or more boats leave before approaching within 300 metres.

7 If a group of whales changes direction repeatedly or changes behaviours quickly (e.g., from slow to fast travelling), these are signs of possible disturbance and the group should be left alone.

8 Aircraft should maintain an altitude of 1,000 feet or move above whales. Float planes should refrain from landing in the vicinity of whales.

Regulations and Licensing

In Canada, the Department of Fisheries and Oceans is responsible for the management and protection of marine mammals, including killer whales. In the United States, the responsible agency is the National Marine Fisheries Service. In both countries, regulations specifically prohibit disturbance of whales. Infractions are subject to fines and/or imprisonment.

Activities such as research or commercial photography may require a license or permit to approach whales. Individuals wishing to undertake such activities should contact the Department of Fisheries and Oceans in Canada, or the National Marine Fisheries Service in the US, to ensure that their proposed activity is permissible and to determine whether or not they will require a permit.

A pilot landed his float plane near the transient male T31 for some whale watching. Landing planes near whales is risky for both aviators and whales and is not recommended.

G. Ellis / Ursus

Right: **Killer whale spyhopping, northern Vancouver Island.**

G. Ellis / Ursus

Left: Killer whale breaching, Alaska.
G. Ellis / Ursus

Right: Group of killer whales at surface.
G. Ellis / Ursus

Below: Member of T18 group leaping during unsuccessful attack on a Steller sea lion, near Port Hardy, Vancouver Island.
J. Ford / Ursus

Left: Transient male T20 foraging in kelp bed, northern Vancouver Island.

J. Borrowman

Right: Minke whale showing clear evidence of a killer whale attack, off northern Vancouver Island.

G. Ellis / Ursus

Below right: Transient male T29 surfacing amidst Inside Passage vessel traffic, Queen Charlotte Strait, BC.

G. Ellis / Ursus

Following page: T73 surfacing with companion, southeastern, Alaska.

D. Ellifrit / NMML

Catalogue of
Transient Killer Whales

In the following sections, we provide an overview, identification guide, and registry for the transient population found in the coastal waters of British Columbia, Washington, and southeastern Alaska. The procedures for assigning whales to this west coast community and naming them are described, as are techniques we use to estimate the age of animals. An identification photograph of each whale is presented, along with its sex, where known, and its actual or estimated year of birth.

Determining Community Membership

Over the past decade, it has become increasingly clear that killer whales, despite belonging to the same single species, live in separate socially isolated populations and communities, each of which is genetically and acoustically distinct. These populations often share the same waters, and it is thus very important that whales be assigned to the appropriate community or population on the basis of clearly defined and consistent criteria.

The main criterion we use to determine the social identity of killer whales is their pattern of association. All whales that can be linked together through their associations form a *community*. Each whale in a community may not necessarily have been observed to mix with the others, but all can ultimately be connected through a network of mutual associates. Thus, if whale A is seen with whale B, and whale B with whale C, all three are considered part of the same community through A and C's association with B.

Within resident communities, stable groups of associating whales are related by matrilineal descent and are organized into pods or subpods depending on the strength of social bonds. Resident pods tend also to have distinctive vocal dialects that further define the group's social identity. Within the transient community of British Columbia, Washington, and southeastern Alaska, associations tend to be less stable. Large pods of maternally related whales do not form because individuals often disperse from their natal group and travel with other whales in the community.

Within the transient community, just as there are no large resident-type pods, there are no pod-specific dialects. Rather, all transients recorded to date share at least a few distinctive calls, and these provide an additional means of identifying members of the community.

With four exceptions (T168 group), all of the 219 transients in this catalogue can be linked together through associations. Ten of these whales have also been identified in waters off California or Oregon, tying in an additional 95 transients catalogued only in that southern region through associations. The total community size is thus about 314, although some whales in the catalogue may well be dead, while others have yet to be identified. Because transients in the California-Oregon region seldom mix with those in the British Columbia-Washington-southeastern Alaska region, they are best considered subcommunities. The "AT1" transients and "Gulf of Alaska" transients identified in the Prince William Sound area, Alaska, are separate communities that have not been observed to mix with each other or with the west coast community.

The Naming System

Because transient and resident societies differ in stability and structure, we have developed different systems for naming individuals and groups in the two populations. To understand how these naming systems evolved, it is best to review the history of our study. In the early stages of our research, any group of whales was considered to be a pod and was given a letter designation when first encountered. Individuals within the pod were assigned a number in the order they were identified. Thus, whale A1 was the first whale identified in pod A, whale A2 was the second identified, and so on. Early encounters involved resident whales, and repeated sightings of these groups often revealed that the first encounter actually involved two or more pods that happened to be travelling together when first identified. These pods were then renamed for distinctive animals in the group; thus, A pod became A1, A4, and A5 pods.

Dialect studies later showed that in most, but not all, cases, pods with the same letter designations were actually closely related kin groups.

For the first 20 years of our study, the naming procedure developed for resident pods was also used for transients. However, from the outset it was evident that the naming system was not ideal for transients. For example, some mature transient males travel alone most of the time, and for consistency these individuals were also given pod status. Because many small transient groups and lone individuals were identified, in addition to the numerous resident pods, the alphabet was quickly exhausted. Transient "pods" were thus arbitrarily given the same letter designation, even though there was no evidence that they were related. This proved to be counter-intuitive for many people, who naturally assumed, for example, that pods Q1, Q3, Q4, and Q9 were more closely related to each other than to pods O5, O10, and O21. The naming system was quickly becoming both cumbersome and misleading.

As it became apparent over the past decade that transients have a different social structure than residents, it was obvious that the resident-type naming system was inappropriate and had to be revised. Unlike residents, transients frequently leave their natal group for long periods of time, or even permanently. After leaving their natal group, they may join another group for several years, then switch to a different group. With the old naming system, individuals became a new pod when they left their original pod. Thus, groups might be composed of individuals from different "pods," each of which would have a different alphabetic designation. Very likely, several of the original "pods" named in the 1970s and 1980s were actually composed of unrelated whales.

In order to resolve this increasingly unworkable and confusing situation, we chose several years ago to rename all transients in our study, using a new naming system. In this system, every whale is given the letter "T" for transient, and a unique number or alphanumeric. Individuals that were born before the study began, or whose mother is unknown or uncertain, are given a unique number. Whales that tend to travel together are given consecutive numbers in most cases. Individuals that are known offspring of identified females are given the same T-number as their mother, plus a letter signifying birth order. Hence, the first known offspring of whale T2 is T2A, the second is T2B, and so on. In subsequent generations, the birth order alternates between numbers and letters. Thus, if T2B becomes a productive mother, her first offspring will be T2B1, her second T2B2, and so on. With this naming system, an individual's maternal genealogy is always encoded in its name, regardless of which group it is travelling with. The usefulness of this naming system can best be appreciated by following the actual story of the T2 lineage, given in the sidebar on pages 20-21.

Catalogue Composition and Organization

All transient individuals identified in British Columbia, Washington, and southeastern Alaska that we consider likely to be alive as of 1998 are included in this catalogue. Because whales often disperse from their natal group and years may pass between resightings of some individuals, it is difficult to be certain when whales are dead or have permanently left the region. We have chosen to exclude most individuals that meet the following criteria: calves and juveniles that disappeared from their natal group when less than five years old; adults that were sighted regularly every year but have not been seen for five or more years; and adults that were sighted infrequently but have not been seen in more than 10 years. Twenty-five identified whales meeting these criteria have been excluded, but it is possible that some of these may be alive and that some individuals shown in the catalogue may in fact be dead.

Whales are arranged in numeric order in the catalogue, from T1 through T172. Mothers and offspring, and other individuals that tend to travel together, are grouped on the same page whenever possible. These groups are named

Transient juvenile T75A surfacing alongside her mother, T75.
D. Ellifrit

either for the matriarch of the group, if it is a known kin group, or after the lowest numbered female in the group. It should be kept in mind that, in many cases, group composition is likely to change as animals change preferred associates, and that groups are not necessarily composed of related individuals.

To assist in whale identification, we have prepared photographs in three size categories that reflect the body size of individuals:

- **Calves and small juveniles** (height of photograph = 4 cm). This category includes young whales, one to three years of age. These small individuals are often difficult to photograph and are usually indistinctly marked.

- **Older juveniles and adult females** (height of photograph = 6 cm). All whales greater than four years of age, except adult males, are included in this category.

- **Adult males** (height of photograph = 8.5 cm). The dorsal fin of males grows rapidly at the onset of puberty, usually around 13 to 15 years of age, and reaches a height of almost two metres at maturity. This category includes males whose fin is part way through this growth spurt or has reached full height.

Sex and Year of Birth

Below each whale's photograph in the catalogue we have indicated its sex, where known, and its estimated or actual year of birth. The sex of mature whales (over about 15 years old) is easy to determine because of the much larger dorsal fin of males relative to that of females. Establishing the gender of juveniles and calves, however, can be quite difficult. If a small whale happens to roll upside down at the surface, and if we are able to get a clear view or photograph of its underside, its sex can be determined from distinctive pigmentation patterns in the genital area and from the presence of mammary slits in females. Unfortunately, we get few such opportunities with transients compared to residents because we spend relatively less time with them.

Our estimates of the year of birth for transients vary widely in precision. For individuals born during the study to transient groups that we encounter regularly, ages can be considered correct unless noted. As with residents, however, most whales are probably born during the late fall to spring period when little fieldwork is done, so we are usually unsure whether a calf is born early in the new year or late in the previous year. To simplify our analysis, we have standardized all births to 1 January for young-of-the-year calves.

For whales born prior to the beginning of the study or encountered for the first time as juveniles or adults, we have used various methods to estimate year of birth. Those individuals that were immature, but not calves of the year when first identified, were aged by their relative size. Juveniles that were older when first seen were aged in reference to the year that they became sexually mature. These birth dates can be considered accurate to within ± 2 years. Whales that were mature when identified were aged by indirect methods. For females, year of birth was estimated from the age of their offspring. However, because offspring may leave their mother's group, there is greater uncertainty in age estimates for transient females than residents. These estimates have potential inaccuracies of as much as 20 or more years, as females may be older than thought. For mature males, it was not possible to accurately estimate the year of birth. Instead, their ages are given as the latest year the whale could have been born, based on an average minimum age of 20 years for physical maturity in bulls.

T2 Group

T1 ♂ 1960

T2 ♀ 1950

T2A ♂ 1972

T2B ♀ 1979

T2C ♀ 1989

The T2 group is one of the best-known transient matrilines. T1, also known as Charlie Chin because of a facial deformity, has not been seen since 1992 and may well be dead. T2A and T2B have both dis-persed from their mother. For the full story on this lineage, see sidebar on pages 20-21.

T7 Group

T7 ♀ ≤1961

T7A ♂ 1976

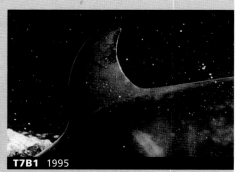

T7B ♀ 1982

T7B1 1995

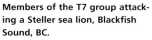

Members of the T7 group attacking a Steller sea lion, Blackfish Sound, BC.

G. Ellis / Ursus

The T7 group is one of the most common and stable groups in British Columbia. It was first seen in 1974 and has been encountered in most years since. It is one of only a few groups that contain a matriline with three generations that still travel together. T7B is one of only a few transient mothers of known age: she was born in 1982, gave birth to T7B1 at age 13, and to T7B2 at age 16 (no photo of T7B2 is yet available). T7 and a presumed offspring, T9, were captured at Pedder Bay near Victoria in 1975. T7 was subsequently released, but T9 and was sent to an oceanarium, and it died in 1990.

T10 Group

T10 ♀ ≤1963

T10A ♂ 1978

T10B ♂ 1983

The T10 group is another well-known transient group in British Columbia, but it has not yet been sighted in Alaskan waters. T10A has not been seen since late 1992, but he may have dispersed from the area.

T11 Group

T11 ♀ ≤1963

T11A ♂ ≤1978

The T11s travel frequently with the T10 group or the T109 group. They also have not been observed in Alaska.

T12 Group

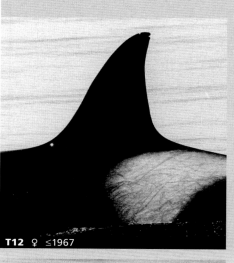

T12 ♀ ≤1967

T12A ♂ 1982

T12B 1985

T12C 1993

The T12 group is most often sighted around Vancouver Island, and occasionally in the Queen Charlotte Islands. T12B may be an emigrant, as it disappeared not long after T12C was born.

T13 Group

T13 ♀ ≤1965

T14 ♂ 1964

T14 is quite likely the son of T13. They have not been seen apart since first identified in 1975. This pair was captured and radio-tagged in 1976. The tags resulted in the distinctive scars seen at the base of their dorsal fins, apparently as a result of the whales' attempts to remove the devices. For the full story of this incident, see opposite page. Although preferring the waters around southern Vancouver Island, the pair has also been sighted once in southeastern Alaska.

Capture and Radio-Tagging of T13 and T14

In March 1976, a group of six transient whales was captured near the head of Puget Sound, Washington, as part of a live-capture operation to supply whales to aquaria. This group included T26 and T27 (see "An Encounter," p. 16, and p. 52), T46 and T47 (p. 56), and T13 and T14. Due to public outcry at the time of the capture, all the whales were eventually released, but T13 and T14 were held for several weeks longer than the others for research purposes.

The two whales were transferred to the Seattle Aquarium, where researchers with the University of Washington designed "radio-packs" to carry VHF tags for tracking each whale after release. These backpacks were fitted to the leading edge of the dorsal fin of the whale and held in place by five stainless-steel surgical pins, each 4 millimetres in diameter. Each pin was bored through the fin and fitted with corrosive nuts, so that the radio-pack would fall off in about a year. The radio tags weighed about 1.5 kilograms each and were designed to transmit for several months and be receivable at ranges of up to 5 nautical miles from boats, or 18 miles from aircraft.

In preparation for release, the whales were moved from Seattle to a small bay on San Juan Island. They were finally released with radios operating in late April 1976, about seven weeks after capture. The whales were then tracked almost continuously by boat for the next 10 days, after which the signals were lost due to radio interference. The radio signals were picked up periodically over the next five months, then the whales disappeared. When the whales were next encountered three years later, we found that they had lost their radio packs, but the surgical pins remaining in the fins had caused a build-up of scar tissue that was clearly visible, especially in T13. Fortunately, these wounds have healed, and the whales have otherwise shown no ill effects of this rather invasive tagging procedure.

Over the 10 days of continuous tracking, the radio tags provided considerable data on dive times and speed of travel. The whales travelled an average of 68 nautical miles per day, at an average speed of 2.8 knots. They reached a maximum speed of 16 knots on occasion, but this was not sustained for long. Three or four short dives as the whales breathed averaged 21 seconds in duration, and these were followed by longer dives averaging 5.77 minutes. The longest dive recorded was 17 minutes. Although this information is interesting, it could have been easily collected through standard observation techniques. Today, modern data loggers and satellite tags can provide far more useful data on dive depths, underwater swimming speed, the locations of whales over a wide range, and so on. Tags can be attached for a few hours using suction cups, but a non-invasive technique has yet to be developed that would allow reliable attachment for long-term satellite tracking of killer whales.

Some of the attachment pins used to secure a radio-tag to T13's dorsal fin remain in the fin's tissue, 21 years after tagging.
J. Ford

Scars from the attachment of a radio tag in 1976 are still visible on T14's dorsal fin.
J. Borrowman

Transient whales T14 (foreground) and T13 with radio tags, San Juan Island, Washington, April 1976.
K. Balcomb

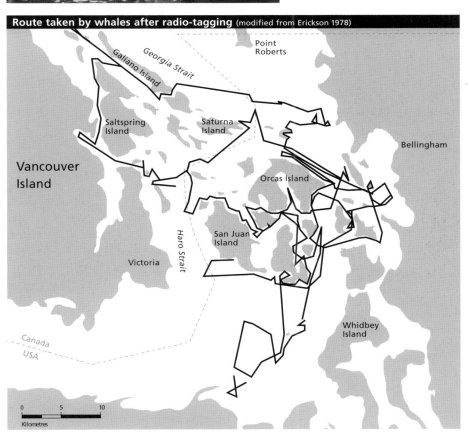

Route taken by whales after radio-tagging (modified from Erickson 1978)

Point Roberts

Galiano Island

Georgia Strait

Saltspring Island

Saturna Island

Vancouver Island

Bellingham

Orcas Island

Haro Strait

San Juan Island

Victoria

Canada
USA

Whidbey Island

0   5   10
Kilometres

T18 Group

Members of the T18 group swimming in 50 knot, −20°C, mid-winter conditions, Douglas Channel, BC.

J. Borrowman

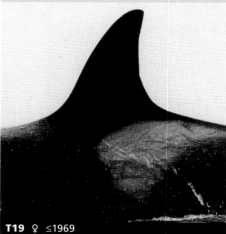

T18 ♀ ≤1974

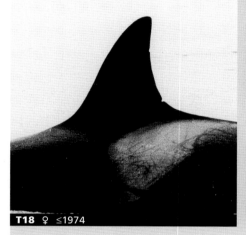

T17 ♀ ≤1964

T19 ♀ ≤1969

T19B ♂ 1995

T17 has not been identified since 1992 and may have died or dispersed from the region.

The T18 group was unknown until first identified in 1984, but it has been encountered in most years since then. This group was observed to drive a Pacific white-sided dolphin onto shore near Port Hardy in 1995 – the dolphin subsequently died.

T21 Group

T20 ♂ ≤1963

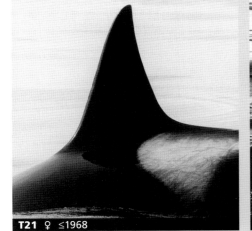

T21 ♀ ≤1968

T22 ♀ ≤1976

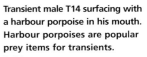

Transient male T14 surfacing with a harbour porpoise in his mouth. Harbour porpoises are popular prey items for transients.

H. Naito

This group was first encountered in 1984 and has been a very common group since then. It has only been sighted around Vancouver Island and along the central mainland coast of British Columbia. The whales in this group were involved in a violent interaction with the resident J pod, described on page 83.

T23 Group

T23 ♀ ≤1965

T24 ♂ 1974

T23C 1990

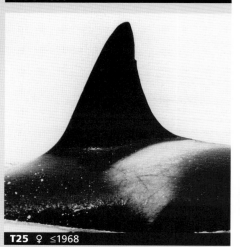

T25 ♀ ≤1968

T26 ♀ ≤1966

T27 ♀ ≤1966

T23D 1993

T26 Group

The T23 group is often sighted along the west coast of Vancouver Island but has also been identified as far north as Glacier Bay, Alaska. Two offspring of T23 – T23A and T23B – died in their first year of life.

T26 and T27 were first identified when captured in Budd Inlet, Puget Sound, along with T13, T14, T46, and T47. They have only been sighted four times, the last in 1991.

T28 Group

T28 ♀ ≤1972

T28A 1994

The T28 group includes T146 (p. 84), who is a probable offspring of T28. The group has only been encountered on 10 occasions, mostly in the Queen Charlotte Islands or southeastern Alaska. The calf T28B, born in 1997, has only been sighted once and no adequate identification photo is yet available.

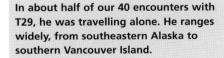

T29 ♂ ≤1956

In about half of our 40 encounters with T29, he was travelling alone. He ranges widely, from southeastern Alaska to southern Vancouver Island.

T30 Group

T30 ♀ ≤1967

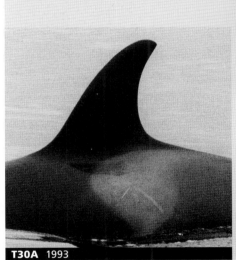

T30A 1993

T30B 1993

The T30s have only been seen six times, off northern Vancouver Island and the Queen Charlottes Islands.

T32 Group

T31 ♂ ≤1954

T34 ♀ ≤1970

T35 ♀ ≤1970

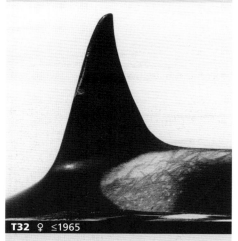

T32 ♀ ≤1965

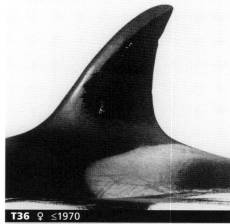

T36 ♀ ≤1970

T36A 1990

T40 ♂ ≤1962

The T32 group formerly included a female, T33, who was a probable offspring of T32. T33 had a calf in 1987, which died shortly thereafter, and she herself disappeared in 1989. T32 has not been seen since 1994 and may be dead. T31 has been sighted travelling alone on several occasions since then.

T34, T35, T36, and T36A are poorly known whales that have been encountered off the west coast of Washington, on the central BC coast, the Queen Charlotte Islands, and southeastern Alaska. T99 (p. 70) and T137 (p. 81) may both be older offspring of T36. These whales are not known well enough for us to be certain whether or not they form a stable group.

T40 is encountered mostly in southeastern Alaska but has also been seen as far south as Victoria, on Vancouver Island. He has a wide range of travelling associates.

Distinguishing Transients and Residents

The most reliable way to determine whether a group of whales is transient or resident is to identify specific individuals by examining their natural markings. This can be done by slowly approaching the group (following the whale-watching guidelines on pp. 31-32), and then carefully examining their dorsal fins with binoculars. Make note of any nicks or scars, then refer to the catalogue section of this book or, for residents, our book *Killer Whales: The Natural History and Genealogy of* Orcinus orca *in British Columbia and Washington State*. Photographs using a telephoto lens and high-speed film, or a video camera recording, may help for later examination and identification.

Often it is not possible to approach a group of whales for individual identification. Passengers on ferries or cruise ships may only have a few minutes for observation as the ship passes, and whale watchers on shore may have similarly brief encounters. In such cases, it is still possible to determine with fair confidence whether the whales being observed are residents or transients. A number of features in the whales' behaviour and appearance can, when considered together, be used to distinguish the two forms.

Group Size

Groups of whales containing less than five whales are usually transients, and groups of more than 10 are most often residents. About 80 percent of all our transient encounters involve six or less animals, and more than 10 transients together is quite rare (about 2 percent). Lone transient males are also commonly encountered. In contrast, residents usually travel in groups of 10 to 20, and larger groups are not uncommon. However, because residents often spread out widely while foraging,

it is easy to mistakenly assume that you have encountered a small group while overlooking other group members travelling in the distance. Residents occasionally can be found in groups of five or less, so group size cannot be taken as an absolute indicator of whale type.

Seasonality

Transient killer whales are found year-round in coastal waters, with no strong seasonal peaks in abundance. Most sightings are in summer and early fall, but this may be due to increased numbers of observers, longer day length, and good weather compared to winter. Residents, on the other hand, show strong seasonality. Resident pods are only common in inshore waters of southern British Columbia and Washington from June through October, corresponding to the timing of salmon migration. Thus, if a small group of whales is encountered in this region from November through April, chances are they are transients.

Appearance

The dorsal fins of residents and transients often differ subtly in shape, especially in adult females, as shown in the photographs to the right. It is important to note, however, that the differences described here are not seen in every individual but are typical of the majority for each form of killer whale.

In residents, the fin tip tends to be rounded and positioned over the rear portion of the fin's base. The leading edge of the fin tends to be straight or curved slightly back. The grey "saddle patch" at the base of the fin may be either uniform in colouration or may contain various amounts of black – the latter are known as "open saddles."

In transients, the tip of the dorsal fin is typically pointed and positioned in the centre above the middle of the fin's base. Also, the midpoint along the leading edge of the fin sometimes has a slight bulge. The saddle patch is typically quite large compared to residents, and open saddles are not found.

Dive Times and Swimming Pattern

Both residents and transients typically make a sequence of several short, shallow dives, followed by one long dive. Long dives of transients are most often 5 to 7 minutes in duration, while those of residents are generally much briefer, at 2 to 4 minutes. Some transient dives may be up to 10 or more minutes in duration, but dives of greater than 5 minutes are quite rare in residents.

While foraging, transients often swim very close to shore and frequently follow the shoreline contour into small bays and narrow passages. Residents also may forage close to shore, but they are more likely to cut across bays and inlets. Transients often make unexpected and sudden course changes, while residents are more likely to maintain a consistent direction of travel.

Dorsal fin usually has rounded tip.

Resident fin

Open saddle, often seen in residents but not in any transients identified to date.

Dorsal fin tip generally pointed.

Transient fin

Saddle patch large and uniformly grey.

T41 Group

T41 ♀ ≤1973

T41A 1988

T44 ♂ 1978

The T41 group has most often been observed on the west coast of Vancouver Island. T44 is a probable offspring of T41.

T46 Group

T46A 1979

T46 ♀ ≤1964

T46C 1994

T46B ♀ 1987

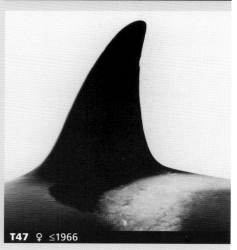

T47 ♀ ≤1966

T46 and T47 were first identified when temporarily captured along with T13 and T14 at Budd Inlet, Puget Sound, in 1976. T122 and T123 may actually be offspring of T46, but a 13-year gap in our sightings of this group precludes confirmation. T46A may actually be the same animal as T122, but a photograph of its eye patch is needed to confirm this possible match. Note the close similarity in appearance between T46 and T86A (p. 67).

T49 Group

T49A 1986

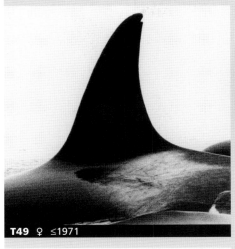

T49 ♀ ≤1971

T49B 1992

T50 ♀ 1980

T51 ♂ 1981

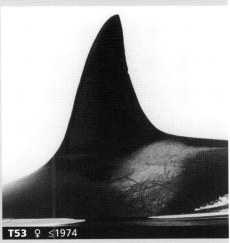

T53 ♀ ≤1974

T50A 1995

T48 is a rather poorly known, roaming male.

T48 ♂ 1975

The T49 group is very wide ranging, as described in "Wandering Whales," on p. 61. T51 only occasionally travels with this group.

T55 Group

T54 ♂ 1972

T55 ♀ ≤1974

T55A 1989

T55B 1994

T56 1982

T57 ♀ ≤1979

T57A 1993

T58 ♀ ≤1976

This group of whales does not travel together as often as it did when first encountered in the mid-1980s.

T59 Group

T59 ♀ ≤1977

T59A 1995

T60 ♀ ≤1980

T60B 1998

The T59 group is known mainly from the north and west coasts of Vancouver Island, and the South Moresby area of the Queen Charlotte Islands. T60 may be an offspring of T59.

Seabirds: Playthings and Practice, or Between-Seal Snacks?

It is not unusual to see transients chasing and harassing seabirds. During most of these incidents, the whales do not seem intent on eating the birds. Rather, they let the bird escape or they abandon it after it has been injured or killed. Seabird harassment appears to be a favourite activity of juvenile transients. The young whales will sometimes swim upside down or on their sides, looking for birds paddling at the surface above. Once a victim is sighted, they will try to slap it with their tail flukes, jump on it, or seize it in their mouth. This interaction may continue for several minutes, before the bird is eaten, incapacitated, or left dead in the whale's wake. We and others have recorded at least 10 seabird species that have become casualties of transients. Frequent victims are common murres, which are flightless for several weeks during the late summer and are like "sitting ducks" for transients. Other species include black brant, common loon, white-winged scoter, surf scoter, cormorant (species uncertain), western grebe, marbled murrelet, rhinoceros auklet, and red-breasted merganser.

Below: **Juvenile transient attempting to catch a rhinoceros auklet, Knight Inlet, BC.** *B. Paterson*

Seabirds seem to be more important as objects of play or harassment than as a dietary item. Juveniles playing with seabirds no doubt learn useful skills in prey capture and handling that may enhance their success in hunting harbour seals and other wily prey. The birds may occasionally be eaten, especially if a whale is hungry, but transients seem not to target birds as a primary quarry. In other parts of the world, killer whales are known to hunt penguins, which are much larger and have more body fat, thereby providing a more worthwhile meal.

Above: **Rhinoceros auklet killed and abandoned in Blackfish Sound, BC, in 1988 by T2B, who was then a juvenile.** *J. Ford / Ursus*

T64 Group

T63 ♂ 1978

T64 ♀ ≤1971

T64A 1993

T61 ♂ 1966

T65 ♀ ≤1971

T65A 1986

T65B 1993

T61 was a subadult when first identified in Tofino in 1977 and was incorrectly assumed to be a female in our 1987 catalogue. He disappeared for 13 years following the 1977 sighting, then was resighted as a lone bull at Langara Island in 1990. Since that sighting, he has turned up with a variety of associates off eastern Vancouver Island, the west coast of Washington, and even in Vancouver harbour.

The T64 group has only been encountered in southeastern Alaska and northern British Columbia.

T66 ♂ ≤1959

T67 ♂ ≤1952

T66 ranges widely in British Columbia and southeastern Alaska, often in the company of T72.

T67 has not been seen since 1985 and may well be dead. He is included here because he is so distinctively marked.

Wandering Whales

Transients are highly mobile whales that are always on the move. In their seemingly continual search for mammalian prey, they can potentially range over wide portions of the coast. Some transient groups seem to have fairly modest home ranges. Several groups are encountered almost entirely along the south coast of British Columbia, with only rare sightings outside this area. Similarly, numerous groups prefer the waters of southeastern Alaska, and seldom, if ever, are seen further south. Others transient groups, however, are far more wide ranging and regularly transit hundreds of kilometres up and down the west coast.

A good example of wide-ranging transients is the T49 group. On 21 June 1995, the group was identified in Glacier Bay, southeastern Alaska. Two weeks later, on 5 July, they were sighted off the west coast of the Queen Charlotte Islands, 700 kilometres to the south, and by early August, they were back in Glacier Bay. Four months later, they turned up near Nanaimo, BC, a distance of about 1,400 kilometres from Glacier Bay. Less than a month after this, on 4 January 1996, they were sighted at Sitka, Alaska, but by early April they were back in British Columbia, off Tofino, Vancouver Island. Thus, in less than 10 months, the T49 group had covered a minimum of 5,000 kilometres of coastline, measured in a straight line. Factoring in typical transient meanderings (they seldom swim on one course for long), the group might well have covered more than double this distance during the period.

Although the T49 group's movements are impressive, the record for coastal coverage is held by T132, T133, T134, and T135. These four whales, known mostly from encounters in Monterey Bay,

California, have also been identified in Glacier Bay, over 2,600 kilometres to the north. Long-distance transits such as this are rarely observed, but there is reason to believe that transients may range more widely than we know. For example, the well-marked male T61 disappeared for 13 years between encounters in 1977 and 1990. It seems unlikely that such a distinctively marked animal would have gone unidentified for this long a period if he was in the region. The continual discovery of new, adult whales in our study area also suggests that whales may range outside the British Columbia to southeastern Alaska coastal region. The T20 group, for instance, is a very common transient group that is sighted many times each year in British Columbia, but was unknown prior to 1984. Where this group resided before this date is a matter of speculation – perhaps they shifted their home range from a remote location in the North Pacific to coastal British Columbia. As killer whale field studies extend into new regions, it is likely that new discoveries of long-range movements of transients will be made.

Above: **Mature male transient T61 surfacing in Vancouver harbour, BC, April 1994.**
J. Ford / Ursus

T68 Group

T68 ♀ ≤1969

T68A ♂ 1984

T68B 1987

T68C 1992

T68D 1997

This productive female and her offspring are known in both southeastern Alaska and British Columbia.

T69 Group

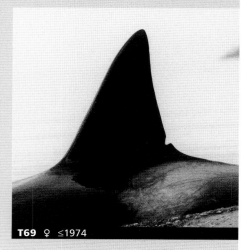

T69 ♀ ≤1974

T69A 1989

T69C 1995

About half of encounters with the T69 group have been in the Queen Charlotte Islands, and the rest around Vancouver Island or the BC mainland coast. A calf, T69B, died in its first year of life.

T71 Group

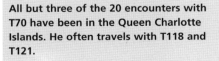
T70 ♂ 1970

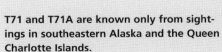
T71 ♀ 1980

T71A 1995

T72 ♂ 1974

All but three of the 20 encounters with T70 have been in the Queen Charlotte Islands. He often travels with T118 and T121.

T71 and T71A are known only from sightings in southeastern Alaska and the Queen Charlotte Islands.

T72 is a mature male encountered mostly in southeastern Alaska but is also seen in the Queen Charlotte Islands and off Vancouver Island. He is occasionally observed travelling as a pair with another male, either T66 or T82.

T73 Group

T73 ♀ ≤1972

T73A 1987

T73B 1991

T74 ♂ 1979

The T73 group is known mostly from southeastern Alaska. T79 frequently travels with this group.

T75 Group

T75 ♀ ≤1976

T75A 1991

T77 ♀ 1981

T77A 1996

These whales are all mostly sighted in southeastern Alaska and make only occasional forays as far south as Vancouver Island. T77 and T78 are probable offspring of T75.

T75B 1994

T75C 1998

T78 ♀ 1986

T78A 1998

Young calf T60B swimming alongside its mother, Johnstone Strait, BC. Note the calf's light grey colouration, which was also seen temporarily in T2C at a similar age.

B. Paterson

Transient female T75 spyhopping alongside her offspring, T75A.

D. Ellifrit

T81 Group

T80 ♂ ≤1967

T83 ♂ ≤1963

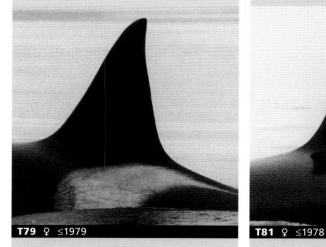

T79 ♀ ≤1979

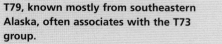

T81 ♀ ≤1978

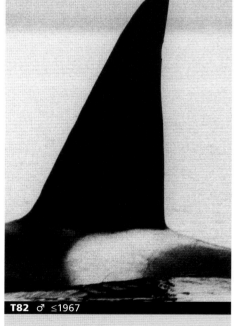

T82 ♂ ≤1967

T84 ≤1974

T79, known mostly from southeastern Alaska, often associates with the T73 group.

T80 and T81 have only been encountered five times to date, each in the Queen Charlotte Islands.

T82 is a wandering male who has been sighted in the Queen Charlotte Islands, southeastern Alaska, and off the north and west coasts of Vancouver Island.

T83 and T84 have only been sighted once in southeastern Alaska in the mid-1980s. They are included here because they are distinctly marked, although they may be dead or have emigrated from the region.

T85 Group

T85 ♀ ≤1977

T85A 1992

T85B 1995

T86 ♀ ≤1973

T86A 1988

These whales have been seen mostly in southeastern Alaska. Note the close similarity in appearance between T86A and T46 (p. 56).

T88 Group

T87 ♂ ≤1963

T88 ♀ ≤1962

T89 ≤1974

T90 ♀ 1980

T89 has not been sighted since 1990 and may be dead or has emigrated.

T91 Group

T91 ♀ ≤1974

T92 ♂ ≤1969

T91 and T92 are poorly known and have been sighted mostly in southeastern Alaska.

Large Whales As Transient Prey

Attacks by transients on large whales in coastal waters of British Columbia, Washington, and southeastern Alaska are rarely witnessed. Rather, transients in these areas seem to focus on smaller mammalian prey, especially seals and porpoises. Transients usually show no interest in large whales they come upon while foraging, and the whales display little or no reaction to the transients. Occasionally, however, the mammal hunters may choose to take on such quarry. Attacks on gray whales are the most frequently observed, perhaps because this species is abundant in nearshore waters during their seasonal migrations. Small, vulnerable gray whale calves appear to be a favourite target. Our colleague Rod Palm, of Strawberry Isle Research Society in Tofino, BC, once observed the T23 group harass a gray whale cow and calf, seemingly intent on killing the calf. To protect the calf from the attacking killer whales, the mother rolled on her back and, with the help of her pectoral flippers, supported the calf on her up-turned ventral side, out of reach of the transients. This defensive tactic seemed to work, and the whales abandoned their intended victim after a few minutes.

On another occasion, the crew of the F/V *Nopsa* watched for almost an hour as a group of seven transients attacked a gray whale cow/calf pair off northern Vancouver Island. Unfortunately, the fishermen had to return to their work before the attack was over, so its outcome is unknown. These transients were likely experienced gray whale hunters, as T164 – the only identifiable whale in the crew's photos – is also known from California, where transient attacks on migrating gray whales are common. Each April and May, transients are observed to attack gray whale

calves migrating northward with their mothers in Monterey Bay, California. Most of these transients have not been observed north of California, and they may be more regular whale hunters than are "local" transients found in British Columbia, Washington, and southeastern Alaska. When attacking gray whales, Californian transients usually work in coordinated groups of 12 to 20, and may take 4 to 6 hours to kill a calf. Gray whale mothers employ various defensive actions to protect their young, including the tactic of holding the calf out of water, described above. They may also swim into the surf close to shore to evade their attackers, or hide in dense kelp beds.

Other baleen whale species that are occasionally attacked in British Columbia, Washington, and southeastern Alaska include minke whales and humpback whales. Minkes are rather small whales, though, at a maximum length of 8.5 metres, they can be larger than full-grown killer whales. They are closely related to the much larger blue and fin whales and share their speedy swimming abilities. Predatory interactions between transients and minkes that we have documented involved brief, high-speed chases, with the minke outpacing its attackers and the transients quickly abandoning the hunt. Sometimes the minkes do not get away, however, as demonstrated by a successful kill observed on the west coast of Vancouver Island in the 1960s (described on p. 27). Also in the 1960s, a minke was apparently driven ashore by killer whales at Schooner Cove on the west coast of Vancouver Island and later shot by local residents. More recently, we came upon a floating piece of minke whale off northeastern Vancouver Island. The numerous distinctive teeth marks on the slab of flesh and its freshness indicated that the minke had been eaten by killer whales not long before we arrived on the scene, but the predators had already disappeared.

Humpback whales are commonly found during summer and fall in nearshore waters of British Columbia and southeastern Alaska, but few attacks have been observed. However, there are other indications that killer whale attacks on humpbacks are not particularly rare. The tail flukes of humpbacks – which are used by researchers to photo-identify individual whales – often bear scars left over from unsuccessful attacks by killer whales. Our colleague John Calambokidis has found that 5 to 10 percent of humpback tail flukes photographed in feeding areas in British Columbia and southeastern Alaska had rake marks caused by killer whale

teeth. This unexpectedly high incidence of scarring suggests that humpbacks often escape from killer whale attacks and that such attacks are more frequent than observations would indicate. Killer whales may "test" many humpbacks, hoping to single out animals that are sick, injured, or old. Because humpbacks migrate thousands of kilometres each year to wintering areas in the subtropics, it may well be that they encounter more predatory killer whales along the migration route, rather than in local summer feeding areas.

Transients attempting to kill a gray whale calf off northern Vancouver Island.
M. Derry

T93 ♂ ≤1969

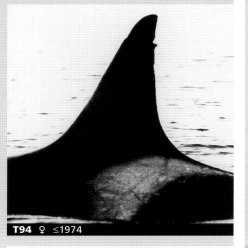

T94 ♀ ≤1974

T95 ♀ ≤1974

T96 ♂ 1971

T97 1980

T99 ≤1984

The whales on this page are seen primarily in southeastern Alaska but have also been identified in British Columbia.

T99 may be an offspring of T36 (p. 54).

T100 Group

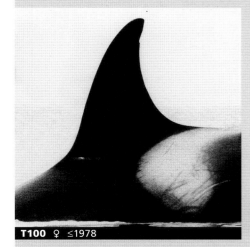

T100 ♀ ≤1978

T100B 1997

T101 ♀ ≤1973

T103 ♂ ≤1968

T101A 1993

T101B 1997

T102 ≤1984

T104 ≤1979

The T100 group is known only from southeastern Alaska. T102 is a probable offspring of T101.

T103 and T104 have been seen only a few times, in southeastern Alaska and the Queen Charlotte Islands.

T105 ♂ ≤1953

T108 ♀ ≤1977

T109 Group

T109 ♀ ≤1975

T109A 1990

T109B 1996

Usually travelling alone, T105 roams widely along the coast. He was one of the first transients photo-identified in our study in 1974. He was mature at that time, which made him at least 45 years old in 1999.

Both T108 and the T109 group were first identified in 1987 and have been seen several times a year since then. They often travel together, although T108 has often associated with the T20 group as well.

T111 Group

T110 ♂ ≤1963

T111 ♀ ≤1975

T111A 1990

T112 ♀ ≤1974

T113 ♂ ≤1975

T114 ♂ ≤1975

T115 ≤1974

These seven whales have only been encountered once in British Columbia, at Langara Island in the Queen Charlottes, in 1990. They are also seen infrequently in southeastern Alaska.

Are Transients or Residents the "Typical" Killer Whale?

We have often asked ourselves this question: Which type of killer whale – resident or transient – is typical of the global species, *Orcinus orca*? In other words, are resident-type killer whales the normal form of the species from which transients have evolved, or vice versa? Or can either be considered to be typical killer whales at a global level?

The answer to such questions is by no means clear. Studies on killer whales in other regions indicate that a wide variety of lifestyles and prey preferences exist in different parts of the world. Off the coasts of Iceland and Norway, large groups of killer whales are found seasonally, where they specialize on herring as their main diet. Along the Patagonian coast of Argentina, a small population

Killer whale snatching a southern sea lion pup from the shallows, Patagonia, Argentina.
J. Ford / Ursus

of killer whales uses a spectacular hunting tactic, involving partial beaching, to prey on southern sea lions and elephant seals. In New Zealand waters, some groups of killer whales hunt stingrays by dislodging them from the sea floor, while in tropical waters, killer whales have been observed feeding on large sharks and sea turtles.

Perhaps the closest parallel to the resident-transient situation may exist in waters around Antarctica. In this region, Russian biologists have described two apparently distinct forms of killer whale that differ in morphology, diet, and behaviour, and have actually proposed a new species on the basis of this distinction. One form is reported to feed primarily on marine mammals and travel in relatively small groups of 10 to 15, while the other form, named *Orcinus glacialis* (or *Orcinus nanus*, depending on the reference source), has a smaller body size, tends to travel in larger groups of 150 to 200, and feeds mainly on fish. This proposed new species has not been accepted within the scientific community because the descriptions were insufficient to warrant such a designation.

It seems probable that in whatever part of the oceans killer whales are found, they have evolved to exploit local prey species that are abundant, predictable, and catchable. However, the evolution of diet preferences is determined by behavioural, rather than genetic, processes. Over time, whales develop specialized hunting tactics for particular prey types, and these become established as behavioural traditions that are passed across generations by cultural transmission. Traditions related to a particular hunting strategy may extend to many aspects of the whales' distribution, behaviour, and social structure. These hunting traditions may become so deeply rooted and pervasive that the whales are culturally constrained from exploiting other prey types to which

they are unaccustomed and from interacting socially with other whales of the same species that hunt different types of food. Social isolation secondarily leads to reproductive isolation, which in turn leads to genetic divergence. This is the most probable scenario that resulted in the evolution of residents and transients on the west coast of North America, and this scenario may have taken place many times in other regions.

It is thus quite possible that neither residents or transients represent the "typical" species, *Orcinus orca*. Rather, a mosaic of distinct, specialized killer whale populations, each socially isolated and genetically discrete, may be found throughout the world's oceans. Some may share the same waters but exploit different prey types, while others may be the sole occupants of certain regions. Some may be highly specialized – like the salmon-eating residents of the northeast Pacific or the herring-eating whales of the north Atlantic – while others are less narrow in their dietary preferences. Some populations may form highly stable societies like residents, while others may live in more fluid groups like transients. Still other populations may well have social structures and behavioural traditions that are unlike anything so far described in the species.

T116 Group

T116 ♀ ≤1977

T116A 1992

T116B 1995

These whales are known only from northern British Columbia and southeastern Alaska.

T117 Group

T117 ♀ ≤1977

T117A 1992

T119 1983

T120 1986

T119 and T120 are probable offspring of T117. The three travel together, but have only been seen on a few occasions.

T118 ≤1979

T121 ♀ ≤1983

T122 ♀ ≤1982

T123 ♀ ≤1982

T121 often travels with T118 and T70. Most encounters have taken place in the South Moresby area of the Queen Charlotte Islands.

T122 and T123 travel with T46 (p. 56) and are likely her offspring.

A member of the T124 group surges out of the water during an attack on a harbour seal near Nanaimo, BC.
G. Ellis

T124 Group

T124 ♀ ≤1967

T124A ♀ 1982

T124A1 1996

T124B 1988

T124C 1992

T124D 1996

T124 is the most productive female in our study, having given birth to four surviving offspring in 14 years. Her first known offspring, T124A, gave birth to her first calf at the age of 14. This group is most frequently seen in southeastern Alaska.

Silence of the Transients:
Cryptic Clicks and Passive Sonar

Lowering a hydrophone into the water in the midst of a group of resident killer whales, one typically hears a variety of strident, scream-like calls, warbling whistles, and staccato clicking sounds. As in most toothed whales and dolphins, calls and whistles are emitted for social communication, and clicks for echolocation. Clicks are usually given in repetitive series, or *click trains*, at rates of a few clicks per second to as high as 300 to 400 per second. These clicks are quite directional and are transmitted ahead of the animal in a narrow beam. When the clicks hit objects in the water, they produce echoes which the whale can use to form an "acoustical image" of its surroundings. Echolocation is likely of great importance to the whales as a navigation aid and a food-finding tool.

Early in our acoustical studies of killer whales along the coast of British Columbia, we became accustomed to the loquacious nature of resident pods. Each pod, we found, vocalized frequently, using a unique vocal dialect that is likely important as an "acoustical family badge" to help pod members maintain contact and preserve the identity of the kin unit. However, it soon became clear to us that transients were far quieter than residents. After dozens of encounters where we monitored the underwater soundscape in the vicinity of transients, we had logged only a couple of hours of active vocalization. The quietness of transients appeared to extend to both social signals and echolocation.

Why should transients be so quiet and residents so vocal? At first, we suspected that the transients might be adopting a "low profile" when in waters occupied by the larger resident pods. This kind of behaviour is used by wolves to avoid detection while transiting territories belonging to other packs. However, transients occasionally do become highly vocal in waters frequented by residents, especially while in the process of killing their prey or following a kill. Almost always when foraging for prey, however, transients are quiet, which suggests that silence might be a hunting tactic.

To examine this question in greater detail, our colleague Lance Barrett-Lennard recorded and compared the underwater sound production, particularly echolocation clicks, of both resident and transient groups in Prince William Sound, Alaska, and along the British Columbian coast. Lance found that, on average, individual resident whales produced echolocation click trains 27 times more often than did transients, and click trains were more than twice as long in residents (7 seconds) than transients (2.8 seconds). The repetition rates in click trains were typically very irregular in transients, but highly regular in residents. Also, transients were found to produce single, or isolated, clicks four times more often than residents. Finally, echolocation clicks of transients appeared to be much less intense than those of residents.

The suppressed, sporadic echolocation of transients, in conjunction with the lack of social signalling during foraging, suggests that the whales are attempting to avoid acoustical detection by their prey. Transients seem to have a "sneak attack" hunting tactic, using the element of surprise to catch prey before it can escape. Unlike fish, marine mammals such as seals and porpoises are sensitive to sound at the high frequencies of echolocation clicks. If the potential prey is alerted to the approach of transients by hearing these clicks, the whales' hunting success would be reduced. Thus, there is a real constraint on the use of echolocation click trains in transients in comparison to residents.

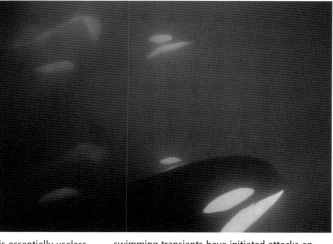

Even though hunting success in transients might be negatively affected by use of resident-type echolocation click trains, success might be even lower without some echolocation. Vision is typically so reduced in turbid coastal waters that it is essentially useless for navigation or detecting objects beyond a few whale lengths away. As a result, transients have developed "cryptic clicks," which provide them with acoustic information necessary to navigate and locate prey, but have qualities that reduce their detectability by wary marine mammals. Isolated clicks and irregular, short click trains seem to be adaptations that camouflage transient echolocation amidst the various ambient noises typical of coastal waters. Snapping and popping sounds are common in the nearshore habitats where transients often hunt. These sounds are created by various invertebrates such as shrimps, mussels, and barnacles. It is likely that seals and porpoises have a difficult time differentiating between these invertebrate sounds and transient echolocation. By using isolated clicks, transients are able to get an acoustic "snapshot" of their surroundings without alerting their would-be prey.

There is growing evidence that transients have another technique for acoustically locating their prey – by simply listening. This so-called "passive sonar" involves cueing on the sounds made by objects in the environment. Seals and sea lions no doubt make splashing sounds as they swim at the surface. Dolphins and porpoises make clicks and other sounds for communication. By swimming quietly and listening intently, transients may be able to pick up these sounds and home in on them with their excellent directional hearing. We have noticed on several occasions that silently swimming transients have initiated attacks on Dall's porpoises, even though the porpoises were beyond visual range. Although the Dall's porpoises do produce echolocation, the frequencies they use are apparently above the hearing range of killer whales, so it may be that the transients were cueing on the swimming or breathing sounds of the porpoises.

Because of the evident reliance of transients on the subtle sounds of their prey or the faint echoes from their cryptic clicks, we are becoming increasingly concerned about the potential impacts of underwater noise on the whales' prey-finding ability. Over the past few decades, many areas along the inside passage have become very busy with noisy, motorized vessels – fishing boats, commercial ships and tugs, cruise ships, whale-watch boats, and so on. This constant man-made noise may very well interfere with the acoustical cues needed by transients to locate prey. This is why we believe it is important that whale watchers stay more than 100 metres from transients and limit their time in proximity to the whales.

Above: **Underwater visibility is often restricted, so transients rely on sound to navigate and locate prey.**
J. Ford / Ursus

T125 Group

T125 ≤1979

T126 ♂ ≤1974

T127 1984

T128 ♂ 1988

The T125 group is uncommon, having been seen only six times in the Queen Charlottes and around Vancouver Island.

Transient male T70 spyhopping near Skedans Island, Queen Charlotte Islands, BC.
C. French

T129 ♂ ≤1971

T130 ♂ ≤1971

T131 ♀ ≤1982

T132 ♂ ≤1968

T133 ≤1979

T134 ≤1979

T135 1985

All the whales on this page are known mostly from the coast of California and Oregon and have been encountered only once outside this region. T129, T130, and T131 were identified off the west coast of Vancouver Island in the company of the T10 and T11 groups. T132, T133, T134, and T135 were encountered in Glacier Bay, southeastern Alaska.

T137 1985

T137 is likely an offspring of T36 (p. 54).

Transient Booms and Busts?

The availability of prey undoubtedly has a major influence on the distribution and abundance of both resident and transient killer whales. The seasonal movements of residents are tied closely to the location and timing of migrating stocks of salmon, which is the preferred prey of these whales. Transients seem to have a less focused diet, feeding on seals, sea lions, porpoises, and whales, but they too are susceptible to changes in prey abundance. Over the years, the impact of humans on the prey of transients may well have caused – and continue to be causing – major effects on transients.

In British Columbia, the primary prey of transients is harbour seals, followed by sea lions. Together, these pinnipeds make up over 70 percent of all attacks and kills we have documented. Harbour seals are preferred partly because they are relatively easy to catch and kill but also because they are the most abundant marine mammal in coastal waters. However, harbour seals have not always been so abundant – in fact, for many years, harbour seals were far less common in coastal waters of British Columbia than they are today. Historically, harbour seals have been considered a nuisance by fishermen because they plunder gillnets for salmon, often damaging the nets in the process. Between 1914 and 1964, the Canadian government paid a bounty for seals, which resulted in an annual kill of about 3,000 seals and served to keep the population suppressed. Then, in the early 1960s, a market for harbour seal skins developed in Europe, which led to a substantial commercial hunt for seals for several years. By the late 1960s, it is estimated that the harbour seal population in British Columbia was reduced to about 10 percent of historical levels.

Steller sea lions in British Columbia did not fare much better than harbour seals during this time. In the early part of this century, thousands of sea lions were shot as a population control measure to reduce perceived negative impacts on commercial fish stocks. Another period of heavy killing took place in the late 1950s and 1960s, when sea lions were used commercially for mink food. By the 1970s, Steller sea lions in BC were reduced to one-quarter to one-third of historic levels, and entire breeding colonies were wiped out.

This dramatic reduction in the density of seals and sea lions must have had an impact on transients, but we will never know its magnitude because no information on transient abundance is available prior to the mid-1970s. Very likely, transients that formerly hunted pinnipeds in the region were displaced to better hunting areas, and the whales may well have been scarce in coastal waters of BC for many years. Possibly the transients shifted to other prey, such as porpoises, which may have affected population levels of these species as well.

By the time our killer whale study was under way in the early 1970s, seal and sea lion killing had mostly ended in British Columbia and numbers were starting to recover. Harbour seals rebounded rapidly at rates of about 12 percent per year during the 1970s and 1980s and may now have reached historic levels of more than 120,000 in BC waters. Steller sea lions have increased more slowly, but they too are making a comeback in the province and are now about twice as numerous as they were 20 years ago. As these prey species have become more common in BC waters, our sense is that transients have as well. However, because of changes in our field research effort and methods over the years, it is difficult to be sure of how great this increase has been.

Although hunting conditions for transients are improving in British Columbia, this is not the case throughout the northeastern Pacific. In western Alaska and the Aleutian Islands, populations of Steller sea lions and harbour seals have declined dramatically over the past 20 years. The causes of this decline are not yet understood, although reduced food availability in the region, perhaps resulting from over-fishing by humans, is often implicated. Because of the decline in seals and sea lions, it appears that mammal-hunting killer whales in the central Aleutians have shifted to hunting sea otters, which are not usually preferred prey but are nonetheless edible. This increase in predation on sea otters is thought to have been responsible for a major decline in the species' abundance in the area, from approximately 50,000 in the 1980s to 12,000 by the mid-1990s. Interestingly, only a few killer whales, feeding solely on sea otters, could have caused a decline of this magnitude.

T139 Group

T138 ♂ ≤1967

T139 ♀ ≤1978

T140 ♀ ≤1982

T141 1985

This group, encountered on only a few occasions in British Columbia, is very poorly known.

T143 Group

T142 ♂ ≤1967

T143 ♀ ≤1978

T144 1983

The T143 group was seen travelling in isolation over several years before finally being observed with known transients, at which point it officially became a member of the transient community.

Residents vs. Transients: Indifference, Avoidance, or Aggression?

For many years, the nature of the relationship between transients and residents has been the subject of much curiosity and speculation. As they both share the same waters, the two forms of killer whales must often come into contact with each other, yet they have never been seen to travel together. They are no doubt aware of each other, but is each indifferent to the other's presence, or does one type avoid the other? Is there any form of communication or interaction and, if so, is it hostile or peaceful? As the late Mike Bigg once joked, it's as if they have a treaty where, by agreement, the two forms feed on different prey and stay out of each other's way.

Seeing residents and transients in the same vicinity is not a common occurrence, but it has been witnessed often enough by ourselves and our colleagues so that a pattern is starting to emerge. Either the two forms pass as if neither notices the other or the transients actively avoid encountering the residents. In cases of avoidance, transients on a "collision" course with a pod of residents deviate from their path and skirt around the residents, or reverse their course in order to stay clear. We have noticed on occasion that transients begin to take evasive action once the underwater vocalizations of an approaching group of residents become audible, at a range of a few kilometres or so. As transients are most often silent when they travel and forage, they may typically go undetected by the larger, vociferous resident pods.

It seemed odd to us that the mammal-hunting transients should be intimidated by fish-eating residents, until an precedented and dramatic incident helped to shed light on a possible reason why. On 13 February 1993, one of us (Graeme Ellis) received a phone call from a waterfront resident in Nanaimo, reporting a group of killer whales. Graeme quickly collected his photo-identification equipment and headed out in his small skiff to intercept the whales. Around 10:30, he encountered 10 members of J pod, a well-known southern resident pod, who were heading south a couple of miles from Nanaimo harbour. Soon after encountering the group, the whales began "porpoising" – swimming at high speed – toward Descano Bay, some two miles distant at the northwest end of Gabriola Island. Graeme ran ahead to investigate where the J whales were headed at such speed, and as he approached the small bay, he sighted more whales, which were creating a great deal of splashing in the water.

Moments later, Graeme arrived in Descano Bay to find more of J pod in a tight group, and they appeared to be in a very excited state. Shortly thereafter these were joined by the previous J group, still travelling at high speed. At 11:00, as the whales began to charge together toward the head of the bay, a group of three transient whales, T20, T21, and T22, suddenly surfaced a few metres ahead of the residents. The transients were clearly fleeing from the larger resident group, and it appeared that the residents were attempting to drive the transients toward and possibly onto the beach. All the whales were extremely agitated, and intense vocalizations were clearly audible through the hull of the boat, even over the noise of the outboard motor. Graeme observed what appeared to be fresh teeth marks on T20's dorsal fin and T22's flank. All ages and both sexes of the resident whales seemed to be involved in the fray. Just as the whales drew near a ferry dock located along the shore, a ferry backed out of its slip and disrupted the interaction. The transient group immediately dove and surfaced near the far side of the bay, followed by the J pod whales about 200 metres behind. About 5 minutes later, the transients left the bay and swam steadily south, with the J's following slowly several hundred metres behind. At

11:35, the transients went through Dodd Narrows, a small tidal channel leading to the south, but J pod did not follow. Instead, they milled about for 25 minutes, when they were finally joined by the female J17 and her newborn calf, J28, who had not been present during the earlier altercation with the transients.

Although the motivation for this apparent attack on the transient group is not known, it is possible that the presence of the very young calf in J pod was a factor. Being mammal-predators, transients may represent a threat to residents in certain circumstances, such as when there is a vulnerable newborn in the group. The aggressive charge may thus have been a defensive action to discourage the transients from approaching the pod. Attacks such as this appear to be rare – this is the only aggressive encounter recorded in over 25 years of study. However, such incidents may occur often enough that transients prefer to give the larger resident pods a wide berth whenever they find themselves in the same vicinity.

T145 ♂ 1972

T145 is the only known transient with a collapsed dorsal fin. He was only seen during 1987-89, from southern Vancouver Island to southeastern Alaska.

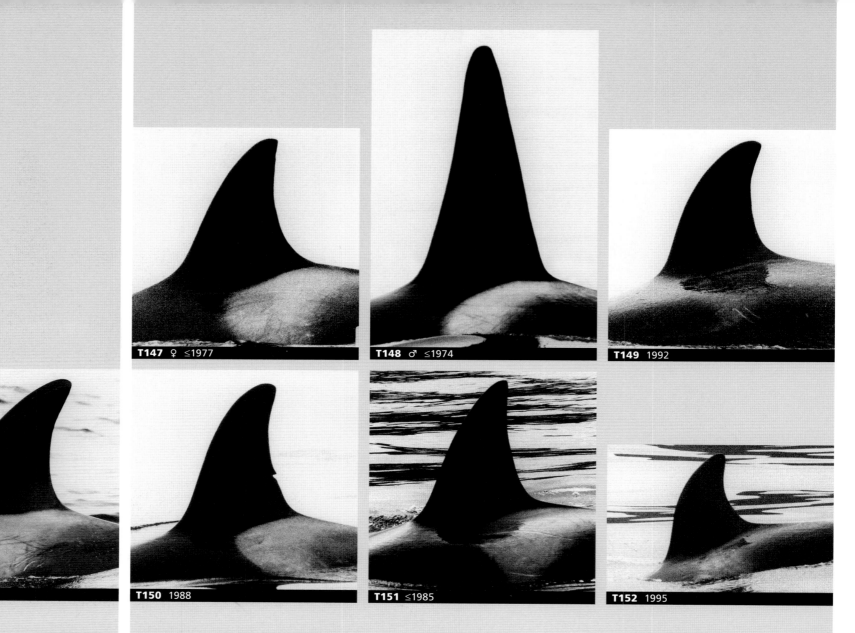

T147 ♀ ≤1977

T148 ♂ ≤1974

T149 1992

T146 1989

T150 1988

T151 ≤1985

T152 1995

T146 is a probable offspring of T28 (p. 53) and has only been observed with that group.

T147 through T152 are rare and have only been encountered in the Queen Charlotte Islands.

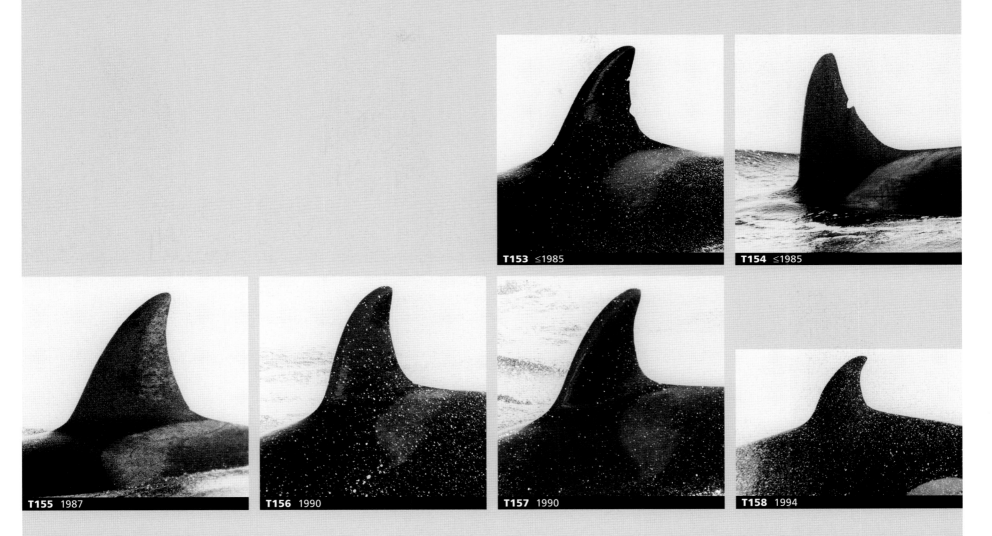

T153 ≤1985

T154 ≤1985

T155 1987

T156 1990

T157 1990

T158 1994

These whales are known only from a single encounter off northern Vancouver Island, where they were sighted with the T13 group and various other transients.

T159 ♂ ≤1973

T160 ≤1984

T161 ≤1984

T162 ♂ ≤1971

T163 ♂ 1975

T159, T160, and T161 are each known in British Columbian waters from single encounters. They have been identified several times in Monterey Bay and other California locations.

T162 and T163 often travel together. They are known from southeastern Alaska and, once, near Vancouver Island.

T164 ≤1985

T164 was identified attacking a gray whale off northern Vancouver Island with six other whales. It also has been documented off Santa Barbara, California.

Toxins in Transients

Although burgeoning harbour seal populations in coastal British Columbia and adjacent waters may be a bounty for transients, all is not well in the food chain. As top-level predators, killer whales ingest a variety of man-made chemical pollutants through their diet. Most important and worrisome of these chemicals are the fat-soluble organochlorines, which include PCBs, dioxins, and furans. PCBs were produced primarily for use in electrical transformers, and although they have been banned for many years, they are extremely persistent and still find their way into the marine environment from old storage sites. Dioxins and furans result primarily from the chlorine-based bleaching process used until recently in pulp mills. These persistent, fat-soluble contaminants enter the ocean and bind to small particles and then work their way slowly up the food chain, from plankton to fish to marine mammals. At each higher trophic level, the concentration of pollutants increases through the process of *bio-accumulation*. Thus, although pollutant levels may be low in individual schooling fish, predators such as harbour seals and resident killer whales feed on many of these, and the fat-soluble chemicals become stored in increasing levels over time in the mammals' blubber. In males, toxin levels increase steadily throughout the animal's life, but in females, levels increase until the individual becomes reproductively active, then drop dramatically. Because these chemicals are fat soluble, they are mobilized from the mother's blubber during lactation and concentrate in her fat-rich milk, then are transferred directly to her offspring through nursing.

Studies on harbour seals in Europe have shown that high levels of PCBs and related contaminants can cause suppression of the immune system, which leads to increased susceptibility to disease,

as well as hormonal and reproductive dysfunction. Some of the harbour seals in Georgia Strait, British Columbia, have been found to have similarly high levels, but of even greater concern are the levels seen in southern resident killer whales. Using biopsy samples collected by Lance Barrett-Lennard and ourselves, our colleague Peter Ross, with the Institute of Ocean Sciences, Sidney, BC, has found that the toxin levels in male southern resident killer whales can be more than five times higher than in Georgia Strait harbour seals. The levels are also higher than in northern resident whales, presumably because southern residents feed in the more polluted waters of Georgia Strait and Puget Sound.

Because transients feed at the top of the food chain – at a higher trophic level than either harbour seals or resident killer whales – it can be anticipated that contaminant levels in these mammal hunters are even greater and may be comparable to levels seen in belugas residing in the highly contaminated St. Lawrence estuary. Such high levels of pollutants in killer whales are cause for serious concern. Although species differences in sensitivity may exist, there is no reason to expect that the kinds of detrimental physiological effects seen in harbour seals would not also take

place in killer whales. This may have an impact on the whale's ability to fight disease, or reproduce successfully. With such a high dose of toxins being transferred to first-born calves through nursing, it may well be that survival of these calves is compromised. Although toxic chemicals such as those described here are banned in many parts of the world, they are still a threat. About 90 percent of all PCBs ever produced are still held in storage, and the security of many of these storage facilities is questionable. It is likely that, without strict controls and monitoring, PCBs and related pollutants will continue to seep into the whales' habitat for years to come.

Above: Pulp mills are the primary source of dioxins and furans in the west coast marine environment. Pinnipeds, such as these sea lions hauled-out on a log boom in front of this pulp mill, accumulate various fat-soluble contaminants in their blubber from their prey. By feeding on seals and sea lions, transients accumulate dangerously high concentrations of such pollutants.
J. Ford / Ursus

T166 Group

T165 ♂ ≤1975

T166 ≤1986

T167 ≤1992

The T165 group has been encountered four times since first identified in 1996, each time in southeastern Alaska.

T168 Group

T168 ♀ ≤1977

T168A ♀ 1992

T169 ♂ 1980

T168B 1997

The T168 group has only been encountered twice, at Langara Island in the Queen Charlottes, and it is the only group of transients not linked through associations to others in the community. It has been determined that they are transients by DNA analysis of a skin sample from one of the whales.

T170 ♂ ≤1973

T171 ≤1984

T172 1989

Scars from killer whale teeth, as well as circular barnacle scars, can be seen clearly on this diving humpback whale near Langara Island, BC.

T170, T171, and T172 are known from only three encounters, twice in the Queen Charlottes and once off the west coast of Vancouver Island. They were not seen before 1994.

Afterword

As we were putting the final portions of this book together in early 1999, a phone call from our colleague and friend, Jim Borrowman, provided a good reminder of why we know as much about transient killer whales as we do, and how we were able to assemble this catalogue of transients. Jim lives in the small community of Telegraph Cove on northeastern Vancouver Island, where he runs a whale-watching company. A skilled photographer and knowledgeable boat operator around whales, he has assisted us for many years in the photo-identification of killer whales. On a recent morning, Jim received a call from a friend in the nearby town of Port Hardy, who reported that a group of killer whales was in the process of attacking sea lions in the bay immediately in front of town. Knowing that sea lion attacks can be drawn-out events, he grabbed his camera case and underwater recording system and made the hour-long drive to the main dock at Port Hardy, where he boarded his friend's boat. Sure enough, the attack was still under way, and by this time a substantial crowd had gathered on the dock to watch the action.

Jim approached the scene of the attack slowly and carefully so as not to disturb the whales, and proceeded to photograph their dorsal fins for individual identification. The four whales had successfully killed a Steller sea lion, estimated by Jim to weigh at least 500 kilograms, and were making repeated dives to feed on the sunken carcass. Although transients tend to be very quiet under water, they are often quite vocal while killing or eating prey. Jim could hear the whales' calls through the hull of the boat, so he lowered his hydrophone over the side and made a tape recording.

While driving back to Telegraph Cove following the encounter, Jim telephoned us to report the event. Listening to his underwater recording over the phone, it was easy to identify the distinctive calls and confirm that the whales were members of the transient community. From Jim's description of the whales' dorsal fins, it wasn't obvious which group of transients was involved. Chances are they were whales that we know and are included in this catalogue, but it is possible that they were individuals that will be new to us. The final answer on the whales' identity will have to await the processing and examination of his rolls of identification film.

We owe much of our understanding of the population structure and natural history of transients to the valuable contributions of a network of friends, colleagues, and associates like Jim Borrowman. Identification photographs, observations of predation, and underwater recordings that are provided by these dedicated and experienced people have helped fill in many of the gaps in our knowledge of transients, especially in remote parts of the coast and during the winter months. However, there are many questions about transients in the region that have yet to be answered. What is the total number of transients in the west coast community and what is the extent of its range? Have newly identified transients in the community immigrated from a distant location or have they simply eluded identification over the first 25 years of our study? How many transient communities exist in the North Pacific and are there related populations in other ocean areas? Answering such questions will take a long time, as well as the continued collaborative efforts of many field workers. As with our book *Killer Whales*, we hope to produce another edition of this book with an updated catalogue of transient whales in five years or so. Hopefully, by then, we'll have a more complete understanding of these intriguing and elusive mammal hunters.

Supplementary Catalogue Information

The following table provides additional information on identification photographs used in the catalogue section of this book. Listed is the year in which identification photos were taken, the photographer of each photo, and his or her affiliation (where appropriate). A key to photographers' affiliations is given at the end of the table. Also given are equivalent names from the former British Columbia naming system and names used recently in other catalogues ("AK ID" are names used by Dahlheim et al. 1997 in southeastern Alaska, and "CA ID" are names used by Black et al. 1997 in California). Finally, dots indicate whether whales have been observed in British Columbia or Washington ("BC/WA"), southeastern Alaska ("SE AK"), and California ("CA"; California sightings are recorded in Black et al. 1997).

Whale ID	Year of Photo	Photographer	Old BCID	AK ID	CA ID	BC/WA Sighting	SE AK Sighting	CA Sighting
T1	1990	D. Matkin	M1	AM1		•	•	
T2	1991	G. Ellis	M2	AM2		•	•	
T2A	1988	S. Baker[1]	M3	AM4		•	•	
T2B	1997	J. Borrowman	M4	AM3		•	•	
T2C	1996	J. Borrowman	M9	AM5		•	•	
T7	1988	G. Ellis	Q1			•		
T7A	1996	C. French[2]	Q2			•		
T7B	1996	C. French[2]	Q10			•		
T7B1	1995	K. Palm[3]				•		
T7B2		no photo				•		
T10	1994	J. Borrowman	Q3			•		
T10A	1989	J. Ford	Q7			•		
T10B	1998	J. Ford	Q12			•		
T11	1987	G. Ellis	Q4			•		
T11A	1995	J. Borrowman	Q8			•		
T12	1994	J. Borrowman	Q9			•		
T12A	1996	G. Ellis	Q11			•		
T12B	1991	J. Borrowman	Q13			•		
T12C	1994	J. Borrowman				•		
T13	1994	G. Ellis	O5			•	•	
T14	1995	J. Borrowman	O4			•	•	
T17	1991	J. Borrowman	O3			•		
T18	1995	G. Ellis	O10			•	•	
T19	1995	G. Ellis	O12			•	•	
T19B	1998	J. Ford				•	•	
T20	1992	G. Ellis	O20			•		
T21	1992	G. Ellis	O21			•		
T22	1997	J. Borrowman	O22			•		
T23	1982	M. Bigg	U1			•	•	
T23C	1998	G. Ellis	U6			•	•	
T23D	1998	G. Ellis				•	•	
T24	1998	G. Ellis	U2			•	•	
T25	1995	D. Matkin	U3			•	•	
T26	1991	J. Borrowman	S3			•		
T27	1990	J. Ford	S5			•		
T28	1995	G. Ellis	S10			•	•	
T28A	1995	G. Ellis				•	•	
T28B		no photo				•	•	
T29	1992	G Ellis	P1			•	•	
T30	1990	J. Ford	P2			•		
T30A	1990	J. Ford	P3			•		
T30B	1995	G. Ellis				•		
T31	1997	G. Ellis	Y1			•		
T32	1994	J. Borrowman	Y2			•		
T34	1994	J. Straley[4]	X1	AV12		•	•	

Whale ID	Year of Photo	Photographer	Old BCID	AK ID	CA ID	BC/WA Sighting	SE AK Sighting	CA Sighting
T35	1980	J. Ford	X2	AV10		•	•	
T36	1996	J. Straley[4]	X3	AM31		•	•	
T36A	1993	J. McCulloch		AM35		•	•	
T40	1994	D. Matkin	T2	AL40		•	•	
T41	1995	G. Ellis	T3			•		
T41A	1995	G. Ellis	T6			•		
T44	1995	G. Ellis	E11			•		
T46	1992	G. Ellis	S1			•	•	
T46A	1979	M. Bigg	S7			•	•	
T46B	1996	A. vanGinneken[6]				•	•	
T46C	1996	D. Ellifrit[6]				•	•	
T47	1992	G. Ellis	S2			•		
T48	1989	D. Matkin	P25	AL5		•	•	
T49	1996	J. Watson	P27	AL7		•	•	
T49A	1996	J. Straley[4]	P32	AL12		•	•	
T49B	1995	J. Watson		AL20		•	•	
T50	1995	J. Watson	P28	AL8		•	•	
T50A	1995	J. Watson				•	•	
T51	1996	J. Straley[4]	P29	AL9		•	•	
T53	1995	J. Watson	P26	AL6		•	•	
T54	1994	T. Smith	P10			•		
T55	1994	G. Ellis	P11			•		
T55A	1994	G. Ellis	P15			•		
T55B	1995	J. Borrowman				•		
T56	1994	T. Smith	P12			•		
T57	1989	A. Morton	P13			•		
T57A	1994	T. Smith				•		
T58	1994	G. Ellis	P14			•		
T59	1997	J. Borrowman	E15			•		
T59A	1997	J. Borrowman				•		
T60	1997	J. Borrowman	E16			•		
T60B	1998	G. Ellis				•		
T61	1992	G. Ellis	V1			•		
T63	1994	D. Matkin	V10	AM20		•	•	
T64	1994	D. Matkin	V11	AM21		•	•	
T64A	1995	D. Matkin		AM27		•	•	
T65	1994	D. Matkin	V15	AM22		•	•	
T65A	1994	D. Matkin		AM25		•	•	
T65B	1996	D. Matkin		AM26		•	•	
T66	1982	M. Bigg	Z1	AQ30		•	•	
T67	1985	M. Bigg	Z50			•		
T68	1997	K. Palm[3]	Z2	AQ10		•	•	
T68A	1995	J. Straley[4]	Z3	AQ11		•	•	
T68B	1997	K. Palm[3]	Z4	AQ12		•		
T68C	1995	J. Straley[4]		AQ14		•	•	

Whale ID	Year of Photo	Photographer	Old BCID	AK ID	CA ID	BC/WA Sighting	SE AK Sighting	CA Sighting
T68D	1997	K. Palm[3]					•	•
T69	1993	K. Heise	M20			•		
T69A	1996	J. Borrowman	M21			•		
T69C	1996	K. Palm[3]				•		
T70	1991	L. Nichol	M25			•		
T71	1994	D. Matkin		AL10		•	•	
T71A	1996	C. Tulloch				•	•	
T72	1997	A. Andrews[1]	Z5	AQ2		•	•	
T73	1990	B. Devine[6]	F21	AQ33		•	•	
T73A	1996	B. Falconer	F22	AQ34		•	•	
T73B	1996	B. Falconer	F23	AQ35?		•	•	
T74	1990	K. Balcomb[6]	F20	AQ32		•	•	
T75	1998	G. Ellis	F15	AQ3		•	•	
T75A	1998	G. Ellis		AQ9		•	•	
T75B	1998	G. Ellis		AQ15		•	•	
T75C	1998	G. Ellis				•	•	
T77	1998	G. Ellis	F17	AQ7		•	•	
T77A	1998	G. Ellis				•	•	
T78	1998	G. Ellis	F18	AQ6		•	•	
T78A	1998	G. Ellis				•	•	
T79	1989	D. Matkin	F19	AQ31		•	•	
T80	1990	J. Ford	M40			•		
T81	1990	J. Ford	M41			•		
T82	1995	D. Matkin	M10	AM30		•	•	
T83	1984	K. Balcomb[6,8]		AL1			•	
T84	1984	K. Balcomb[6,8]		AL2			•	
T85	1994	D. Matkin		AL3		•	•	
T85A	1994	D. Matkin		AL17		•	•	
T85B	1997	J. Doherty[1]				•	•	
T86	1994	D. Matkin		AL4		•	•	
T86A	1997	D. Matkin		AL15		•	•	
T87	1996	D. Matkin		AO1		•	•	
T88	1994	D. Matkin		AO2		•	•	
T89	1988	S. Baker[1]		AO3		•	•	
T90	1997	G. Ellis		AO4		•	•	
T91	1991	J. Jacobsen		AQ4			•	
T92	1989	J. Straley[1,5]		AQ1			•	
T93	1994	D. Matkin		AH1			•	
T94	1996	D. Matkin		AH2			•	
T95	1995	D. Matkin		AH3		•	•	
T96	1995	D. Matkin		AH4		•	•	
T97	1995	D. Matkin		AH5		•	•	
T99	1994	J. Straley[4]		AM34		•	•	
T100	1995	D. Matkin		AL41			•	
T100B	1997	A. Andrews[1]					•	

Whale ID	Year of Photo	Photographer	Old BCID	AK ID	CA ID	BC/WA Sighting	SE AK Sighting	CA Sighting
T101	1995	D. Matkin		AL42			•	
T101A	1995	D. Matkin		AL45			•	
T101B	1997	A. Andrews[1]					•	
T102	1995	D. Matkin		AL43			•	
T103	1994	J. Straley[4]		AM23		•	•	
T104	1989	D. Matkin		AM24		•	•	
T105	1998	Adam U[3]	F1	F1		•	•	
T108	1992	J. Borrowman	E12			•		
T109	1995	G. Ellis	E10			•		
T109A	1996	J. Borrowman				•		
T109B	1996	J. Borrowman				•		
T110	1990	J. Ford		AA1		•	•	
T111	1990	J. Ford		AA2		•	•	
T111A	1990	J. Ford		AA7		•	•	
T112	1990	J. Ford		AA3		•	•	
T113	1990	J. Ford		AA4		•	•	
T114	1990	J. Ford		AA5		•	•	
T115	1990	J Ford		AA6		•	•	
T116	1996	J. Straley[4]		AM33		•	•	
T116A	1998	D. Matkin		AM36		•	•	
T116B	1998	D. Matkin		AM37			•	
T117	1990	J. Ford				•		
T117A	1992	G. Ellis				•		
T118	1991	L. Nichol				•		
T119	1990	J. Ford				•		
T120	1990	J. Ford				•		
T121	1993	G. Ellis				•		
T122	1992	G. Ellis				•	•	
T123	1992	G. Ellis				•	•	
T124	1997	G. Ellis		AL13		•	•	
T124A	1997	G. Ellis		AL14		•	•	
T124A1	1997	G. Ellis				•	•	
T124B	1997	G. Ellis		AL16		•	•	
T124C	1997	G. Ellis		AL18		•	•	
T124D	1997	G. Ellis				•	•	
T125	1994	G. Ellis		AV52		•	•	
T126	1994	G. Ellis		AV50		•	•	
T127	1994	G. Ellis		AV53		•	•	
T128	1994	G. Ellis		AV51		•	•	
T129	1992	R. Palm[3]			CA52	•		•
T130	1992	R. Palm[3]			CA59	•		•
T131	1992	R. Palm[3]				•		
T132	1989	J. Straley[1,5]		AO10	CA20	•	•	•
T133	1989	J. Straley[1,5]		AO11	CA18	•	•	•
T134	1989	J. Straley[1,5]		AO12	CA54	•	•	•
T135	1989	J. Straley[1,5]		AO13	CA27	•	•	•
T137	1993	J. McCulloch		AM32		•	•	
T138	1993	J. Ford				•		
T139	1993	J. Ford				•		
T140	1993	J. Ford				•		
T141	1993	J. Ford				•		
T142	1994	G. Ellis				•		
T143	1994	G. Ellis				•		
T144	1994	G. Ellis				•		
T145	1987	J. Borrowman	X10			•	•	
T146	1995	G. Ellis				•	•	
T147	1995	J. Watson	M31			•		
T148	1995	J. Watson	M30?			•		
T149	1995	J. Watson				•		
T150	1995	J. Watson				•		
T151	1995	J. Watson				•		
T152	1995	J. Watson				•		
T153	1995	K. Heise				•		
T154	1995	K. Heise				•		
T155	1995	K. Heise				•		
T156	1995	K. Heise				•		
T157	1995	K. Heise				•		
T158	1995	K. Heise				•		
T159	1994	J. Calambokidis[7]			CA73	•		•
T160	1994	J. Calambokidis[7]			CA28	•		•
T161	1994	J. Calambokidis[7]			CA38	•		•
T162	1996	J. Straley[4]		AV1		•	•	
T163	1996	J. Straley[4]				•	•	
T164	1995	M. Derry			CA122	•		•
T165	1996	J.Straley[4]				•		
T166	1996	J. Straley[4]				•		
T167	1996	J. Straley[4]				•		
T168	1997	G. Ellis				•		
T168A	1997	G. Ellis				•		
T168B	1997	G. Ellis				•		
T169	1997	G. Ellis				•		
T170	1994	B. Falconer				•		
T171	1994	B. Falconer				•		
T172	1996	J. Darling[9]				•		

1 Glacier Bay National Park, AK
2 Laskeek Bay Conservation Society, Queen Charlotte City, BC
3 Strawberry Isle Research Society, Tofino, BC
4 J. Straley Investigations, Sitka, AK
5 National Marine Mammal Laboratory, NOAA, Seattle, WA
6 Center for Whale Research, Friday Harbor, WA
7 Cascadia Research Collective, Olympia, WA
8 Courtesy of Sea World, Inc.
9 West Coast Whale Research Foundation, Vancouver, BC

Glossary

The following are definitions of some of the terms used in killer whale research and in this book.

breach
occurs when a whale leaps out of the water, exposing two-thirds or more of its body.

bull
a sexually mature male; can be identified by its large size and tall dorsal fin, which is at least 1.4 times taller than its width at the base; bulls reach physical maturity at about 20 years of age.

calf
a newborn or young-of-the-year whale.

clan
one or more pods of resident killer whales that share a related dialect; pods within a resident clan have probably descended from a common ancestral group and therefore are likely more closely related to each other than to pods from other clans. Transients in the west coast community tend to share a common set of discrete calls and are thus equivalent to a single resident clan.

community
killer whales that can be linked together through associations form a community. Although all whales in a community may not have been observed to mix, all can be linked together through intermediate associates.

dialect
a unique set of discrete calls made by an individual whale and its fellow group or pod members; dialects differ among resident pods, but individuals and groups within the west coast transient community share generally the same distinctive set of discrete calls and have little dialect variation.

discrete call
a type of communication vocalization that sounds the same each time it is produced; on average, resident killer whale pods produce about 12 different types of discrete calls, while transient groups produce about half that number.

echolocation
the process by which killer whales and other toothed cetaceans use vocalizations to obtain information about their surroundings; similar to SONAR, echolocation involves the production of high-frequency clicks that echo off objects in the whale's path.

encounter
an occasion when one or more identifiable individual whales have been located.

eye patch
the elliptically-shaped white patch located above and behind a killer whale's eye.

flukes
the horizontal projections forming the tail of the whale.

haul-out
a rocky reef or beach where seals or sea lions climb out of the water to rest.

hydrophone
an underwater microphone used to listen to and record whale vocalizations.

juvenile
an immature whale of either sex.

leapfrogging
a whale-watching practice involving the repeated placement of a boat directly in the whale's path; may contribute to more underwater noise and disturbance than other whale-watching techniques.

maternal genealogy
a family tree showing the ancestry of an individual through its mothers relatives; also known as a matriline.

matrilineal group
a group of whales linked by maternal descent; the basic social unit of resident killer whales, and a common social grouping in transient killer whales. Unlike residents, transient individuals often leave the matrilineal group for extended periods or permanently to travel with unrelated whales.

offshore killer whales
a little-known population of killer whales found mostly in offshore waters off British Columbia but also identified in California, Washington, and southeastern Alaska; more closely related genetically to residents than to transients; appear to travel in generally larger groups than residents or transients.

pod
in resident killer whales, a group of maternally related individuals that tend to travel together; in transient killer whales, the term "group" is used in preference to "pod" because groups are not necessarily made up of related animals.

resident killer whales
a form of killer whale that feeds preferentially on fish, especially salmon, and has a very stable social structure.

saddle
the grey pigmented area at the posterior base of the dorsal fin.

sprouter
an adolescent male whose fin is undergoing a rapid spurt of growth; this usually takes place around 15 years of age.

spyhop
a behaviour where a whale raises its head vertically above the water, then slips back below the surface; a spyhop seems to be a means of obtaining a view above the surface.

subpod
one or more matrilineal groups of resident killer whales that temporarily separate as a unit from a pod; term not relevant to transient killer whales.

transient killer whales
a form of killer whales that feeds preferentially on marine mammals and has a looser social structure than that of residents; transients also differ from residents in dorsal fin shape, group size, behaviour, vocalizations, and genetics.

Bibliography

Baird, R.W., and L.M. Dill. 1995. Occurrence and behaviour of transient killer whales: seasonal and pod-specific variability, foraging, and prey handling. *Can. J. Zool.* 73:1300-11.

—. 1996. Ecological and social determinants of group size in *transient* killer whales. *Behav. Ecology* 7:408-16.

Barrett-Lennard, L.G., J.K.B. Ford, and K.A. Heise. 1996. The mixed blessing of echolocation: differences in sonar use by fish-eating and mammal-eating killer whales. *Anim. Behav.* 51:553-65.

Berzin, A.A., and V.L. Vladimirov. 1983. A new species of killer whale (Cetacea, Delphinidae) from Antarctic waters. *Zool. Zh.* 62:287-95.

Bigg, M.A., G.M. Ellis, J.K.B. Ford, and K.C. Balcomb. 1987. *Killer Whales: A Study of Their Identification, Genealogy and Natural History in British Columbia and Washington State.* Phantom Press, Nanaimo, BC. 79 pp.

Bigg, M.A., P.F. Olesiuk, G.M. Ellis, J.K.B. Ford, and K.C. Balcomb, III. 1990. Social organization and genealogy of resident killer whales (*Orcinus orca*) in the coastal waters of British Columbia and Washington State. *Rep. Int. Whal. Commn.,* Special Issue, 12:383-405.

Black, N.A., A. Schulman-Janiger, R.L. Ternullo, and M. Guerrero-Ruiz. 1997. Killer whales of California and western Mexico: a catalog of photo-identified individuals. NOAA-TM-NMFS-SWFSC-247. Southwest Fisheries Science Center, Nat. Mar. Fish. Serv., NOAA, La Jolla, CA. 174 pp.

Carl, G.C. 1959. Albinistic killer whales in British Columbia. *BC Prov Mus Nat Hist Anthropol Rep (1959)*:29-36.

Dahlheim, M.E. 1997. A photographic catalog of killer whales, *Orcinus orca*, from the central Gulf of Alaska to the Southeastern Bering Sea. NOAA Tech. Rep. NMFS 131, Seattle, WA. 54 pp.

Dahlheim, M.E., D.K. Ellifrit, and J.D. Swenson. 1997. *Killer Whales of Southeast Alaska: A Catalogue of Photo-identified Individuals.* National Marine Mammal Laboratory, Nat. Mar. Fish. Serv., NOAA, Seattle, WA. 79 pp.

Ellis, G. 1987. Killer whales of Prince William Sound and Southeast Alaska: a catalogue of individuals photoidentified, 1976-1986. Hubbs Sea World Research Institute, San Diego, Tech. Rep. NO. 87-200. 76 pp.

Erickson, A.W. 1978. Population studies of killer whales (*Orcinus orca*) in the Pacific Northwest: a radio-marking and tracking study of killer whales. Marine Mammal Commission, Washington, DC. 31 pp.

Felleman, F.L., J.R. Heimlich-Boran, and R.W. Osborne. 1991. The feeding ecology of killer whales (*Orcinus orca*) in the Pacific Northwest. In K. Pryor and K.S. Norris (eds.), *Dolphin Societies: Discoveries and Puzzles*, pp. 113-47. University of California Press, Berkeley, CA.

Ford, J.K.B. 1989. Acoustic behaviour of resident killer whales (*Orcinus orca*) off Vancouver Island, British Columbia. *Can. J. Zool.* 67: 727-45.

—. 1991. Vocal traditions among resident killer whales (*Orcinus orca*) in coastal waters of British Columbia. *Can. J. Zool.* 69:1454-83.

Ford, J.K.B., G.M. Ellis, and K.C. Balcomb. 1994. *Killer whales: The Natural History and Genealogy of* Orcinus orca *in the Waters of British Columbia and Washington State.* UBC Press, Vancouver, BC. 102 pp.

Ford, J.K.B., G.M. Ellis, L. Barrett-Lennard, A. Morton, R. Palm, and K.C. Balcomb. 1999. Dietary specialization in two sympatric populations of killer whales (*Orcinus orca*) in coastal British Columbia and adjacent waters. *Can. J. Zool.,* in press.

Ford, J.K.B., G.M. Ellis, and L. Nichol. 1992. Killer whales of the Queen Charlotte Islands: a preliminary study of the abundance, distribution and population identity of *Orcinus orca* in the waters of Haida Gwaii. Report prepared for Gwaii Haanas/South Moresby National Park Reserve, Parks Canada, Queen Charlotte City, BC, by the Vancouver Aquarium. 69 pp.

Ford, J.K.B., K. Heise, L.G. Barrett-Lennard, and G.M. Ellis. 1994. Killer whales and other cetaceans of the Queen Charlotte Islands/Haida Gwaii. Report prepared for Gwaii Haanas/South Moresby National Park Reserve, Parks Canada, Queen Charlotte City, BC, by the Vancouver Aquarium. 46 pp.

Goley, P.D., and J.M. Straley. 1994. Attack on gray whales (*Eschrichtius robustus*) in Monterey Bay, California, by killer whales (*Orcinus orca*) previously identified in Glacier Bay, Alaska. *Can. J. Zool.* 72:1528-30.

Guinet, C. 1992. Predatory behaviour of killer whales (*Orcinus orca*) around the Crozet Islands. *Can. J. Zool.* 70:1656-67.

Hancock, D. 1965. Killer whales attack and kill a minke whale. *J. Mammal.* 46:341-42.

Heimlich-Boran, J.R. 1988. Behavioral ecology of killer whales (*Orcinus orca*) in the Pacific Northwest. *Can. J. Zool.* 66:565-78.

Heyning, J.E., and M.E. Dahlheim. 1988. *Orcinus orca.* Mammalian Species 304. Amer. Soc. Mammalogists 15:1-9.

Heise, K., G. Ellis, and C. Matkin. 1991. *A Catalogue of Prince William Sound Killer Whales.* North Gulf Oceanic Society, Homer, AK. 51 pp.

Hoelzel, A.R., and G.A. Dover. 1990. Genetic differentiation between sympatric killer whale populations. *Heredity* 66:191-95.

Hoyt, E. 1981. *Orca: The Whale Called Killer*. E.P. Dutton, New York, NY. 287 pp.

Iñiguez, M.A. 1993. *Orcas de la Patagonia, Argentina*. Propulsora Literaria, Buenos Aires. 88 pp.

Jefferson, T.A., P.J.F. Stacey, and R.W. Baird. 1991. A review of killer whale interactions with other marine mammals: predation to co-existence. *Mammal Rev*. 21:151-80.

Kirkevold, B.C., and J.S. Lockard (eds.) 1986. Behavioral biology of killer whales. *Zoo Biology Monographs*, Vol. 1. Alan R. Liss, New York. 457 pp.

Matkin, C.O. 1994. *An Observer's Guide to the Killer Whales of Prince William Sound*. Prince William Sound Press, Valdez, AK.

Matkin, C.O., G.M. Ellis, M.E. Dahlheim, and J. Zeh. 1994. Status of killer whales in Prince William Sound, 1985-1992. In T.R. Loughlin (ed.), *Marine Mammals and the Exxon Valdez*, pp. 141-62. Academic Press, New York.

Matkin, C.O., and E.L. Saulitis. 1994. Killer whale (*Orcinus orca*) biology and management in Alaska. Marine Mammal Commission, Washington, DC. Contract Number T75135023.

Morton, A.B. 1990. A quantitative comparison of the behavior of resident and transient forms of the killer whale off the central British Columbia coast. *Rep. Int. Whal. Comm.*, Special Issue, 12:245-48.

Nichol, L.M., and D.M. Shackleton. 1996. Seasonal movements and foraging behaviour of northern resident killer whales (*Orcinus orca*) in relation to the inshore distribution of salmon (*Oncorhynchus* spp.) in British Columbia. *Can. J. Zool*. 74:983-91.

Olesiuk, P.F., M.A. Bigg, and G.M. Ellis. 1990. Life history and population dynamics of resident killer whales (*Orcinus orca*) in the coastal waters of British Columbia and Washington State. *Rep. Int. Whal. Comm.*, Special Issue, 12:209-42.

Pike, G.C., and I.B. MacAskie. 1969. Marine mammals of British Columbia. *Fish. Res. Bd. Canada Bull*. 71:1-54.

Similä, T., J.C. Holst, and I. Christensen. 1996. Occurrence and diet of killer whales in northern Norway: seasonal patterns relative to the distribution and abundance of Norwegian spring-spawning herring. *Can. J. Fish. Aquat. Sci*. 53:769-79